In His

Presents

Judy Wallace

**Baptist
Publishing
House**

In His Presents
Baptist Publishing House
ISBN 0-89114-341-6

All Scripture quotations unless otherwise noted are from the *Holy Bible, King James Version.*

Copyright © 2002 by Baptist Publishing House. All rights reserved. No part of this publication may be reproduced or transmitted in any form or by any means, electronic or mechanical, including photocopy, recording, or any information storage and retrieval system, without permission in writing from the publisher. Requests for permission to make copies of any part of the work should be mailed to: Permissions, Baptist Publishing House, Post Office Box 7270, Texarkana, Texas 75505-7270.

Printed in the United States of America

Dedication

This book is lovingly dedicated to the memory of my late parents, Doyle Warren and Bernice Cobb Bates.

They gave me:

The Gift of Love,
for each other and for me;

The Gift of a Godly Heritage
for me to pass on to my children;

The Gift of Salvation
by leading me to the Lord during a family devotional

and

The Gift of Their Prayers
that, without a doubt, God is still honoring to this day.
Psalm 16:6
Proverbs 20:7

Table of Contents

Acknowledgments

It is December 19, 2000, 12:15 p.m. I have just finished the last word of the last chapter of my first (and probably last!) book. My feelings are difficult to describe. This has been a labor of love. As someone shared with me, writing a book is like raising a child. It is really difficult to know when to let it go. I really didn't want to start it, but now that it's over I really didn't want to stop.

I wondered at the beginning of this journey why the WMA committee selected authors so far in advance. Now I know. It takes one year for it to sink in that you are supposed to be writing a book. It takes one year to decide for sure what you want to write about. And it takes the third year to actually do the writing.

This isn't a one-person chore. So many people have done so many things to make this possible that I cringe to think I may leave some out. Please know that if I do, God knows the part they played and I will be forever grateful to Him for using them to bless my life.

Thank you

Ruby Poteet and Lucille Hutto for asking me to do this in the first place. I'm not sure you ever answered the question, "Why me?" but God did.

National WMA for electing me to do this. Don't ever take lightly the tremendous undertaking this task is and always remember your authors in prayer. I will never look at a WMA study book quite the same way again.

Paul M. Bearfield, my former pastor and the first one to make me realize the importance of the spiritual gifts. I will never forget you, Brother Paul, and all that you taught me.

Jerry Goodwin, my present pastor who overlooked

my *cutesy* stories and read through this book for doctrinal soundness. Thank you for your strict adherence to God's Word.

Tammie Howell, a dear friend and fellow church member who went through the manuscript for readability. Tammie is a journalism major, but I value her opinion greatly because we are so much alike. Go Sanguine/Cholerics!

Sandra Weihe, a former youth in our church who is now a married woman and teaches English in Wynne, Arkansas. Hers was the most difficult job — correcting my grammar. She was willing to undertake it even after she had just finished doing the same thing with her husband's doctoral dissertation. (I bet mine was a little bit lighter reading, huh Sandra?)

All of the ladies in our Wednesday night class at Worden Baptist Church. They were my guinea pigs and faithfully sat through each class as I taught this book before I wrote it. Some even did all of their homework assignments. You mean more to me than I could ever express.

Bonnie Goodwin, our pastor's wife who gave up her Wednesday night class so I could teach this. I really don't think she minded *too* much.

Worden Baptist Church, for keeping me on the prayer list, encouraging me in this undertaking, and actually praying for me on a weekly basis. You will never know what an important part you all play in my life.

Jenny Lee, my precious sister. You have always been the epitome of a Christian woman. Thank you for letting me retreat to your beautiful home to type the majority of this book while you were gone. I know you have been praying for me too. I love you so much and will always be grateful that you were the oldest.

The sisters at Wynne. I won't even try typing all of your names, but you know who you are. You have no idea how your family has been an encouragement to me over these last few years. I'm grateful the Lord allowed our paths to cross.

Pat Quesenbury. When I told you I didn't know how to write, you simply told me to write like I talked. Now if Jerome Cooper had heard that he might have had fear in his heart. This could have been the size of *War and Peace*!

Jerome Cooper. Bless your heart! How many frantic women have you had to talk through this experience? But every time I called you calmly answered my questions and allayed my fears. Thank you.

Cherita Geraldson. Thank you for letting me know that what I was going through was normal. That helped so much.

The *Prayer Angel* lady from the Missouri Fall Conference of 1999. I am so sorry I didn't get your name, but I have kept your angel on my kitchen windowsill this entire time. Every time I went to the sink, I knew someone was praying for me and this book.

My precious family. Tommy, Jared, and Jill, I truly consider you God's gifts to my life. You have loved me, prayed for me, encouraged me, and let me leave you for a typing sabbatical. I am so blessed to have had the privilege of being part of your home and your lives. Jared, you have added our precious Sally to the family and I am thankful you followed God's leading in the selection of your mate. Jill, if the Lord allows, by the time this is published you should be Mrs. Michael Harrison Mott. He will be a godly mate, one well suited to your temperament. Without his computer expertise, I might never have met my deadline! You are all everything a mother could have hoped for and your mates have truly been prayed for by parents and grandparents alike.

It has been a blessing for me to have written this book. Now may I share with you the three things I asked people to pray for as I went through this process:

- Quality quiet time to study, pray, and write;
- A total filling of God's Spirit so these will be His words and not mine;
- God's anointing on this book that it will touch lives and draw women into a closer relationship with Him.

Only eternity will tell the full extent of His answer.

In Him,
Judy Wallace
Exodus 4:12

Preface

When you hear the phrase *in His presence* or *in the presence of God*, what comes to your mind? Is it abiding in Christ? Is it being in an intimate relationship with our heavenly Father? Is it staying acutely aware and conscious of the fact that God goes *before* us to lead the way; walks *beside* us to comfort and encourage us in our journey; and goes *behind* us to guard and protect us from the enemy?

Many of you have probably taken some type of musical lessons. I took piano lessons. I desperately wanted to learn how to play, but in order to do so I had to practice. Practicing was not fun, it was hard work! When I would sit at the piano for an hour going over the pieces I was to learn, I considered that practice. Not so. Practicing meant that when I came to a section that was difficult or one where I kept making mistakes, I was to stop and concentrate on that one spot until it became smooth and I could play it more easily. It took a conscious decision to focus on that area.

That is the way it is with practicing the presence of God. It takes time. It takes concentration. It takes a focus on the fact that although Jesus is not physically with us today, He is spiritually within us. The more we are consciously aware of that fact, the more we will actually feel the power of being *in His presence.*

What if Jesus were still with us in the flesh today? Would we act differently, dress differently, talk differently, or think differently? His disciples had that privilege. Daily, they were with Him. Daily, they sat and listened to Him in person as He shared His Father's heart and set about to do His will. Daily, they watched how He acted and reacted to the situations that confronted Him. So they, of course, had it all together, right? Wrong! They had doubts. They had heartaches. They had troubles and worries. They went through storms and persecutions. And at times they failed.

Can't you feel our Lord's heart as He says to Philip, *"Have I been so long time with you, and yet hast thou not known me, Philip?"* (John 14:9). Is He saying that to you? Have you been His child for months, years, even decades and yet failed to really *know* Him? Do you go through each day with doubts, worries, and failures and wonder where He is in all of this? That's where you must stop and practice. Focus on the Father and concentrate on the fact that He is not just with us, He is within us.

I spent sixteen years as a teacher and administrator in public education. While there I learned that some students are visual learners, some are auditory learners, and some are kinesthetic learners. In other words, some of us learn by seeing, others by hearing, and still others by doing. We want God to *show* Himself to us. We want to *hear* Him speak to us audibly. We want Him to *do* something so His presence will be more real to us.

Well, He has. He shows Himself to us in a myriad of ways if we will just look for them. He speaks to us through various means if we will just listen for Him. He has His sovereign hand on every aspect of our lives if we will just be consciously aware of Him. In other words, we must *practice* His presence.

That's what this book is about. I want us to know what it is like to be *in His presence* by examining what is *in His presents*! Since some of us are visual learners, I want us to open up the gifts God has given to us and see what's inside. I want us to listen to the crackling paper as we unwrap them and hear His heart in all that is around us. I want us to take off the lids and by doing so be consciously and consistently aware of His presence with us.

Don't we love getting gifts? I know I do. In fact, I've often thought that I probably married the wrong time of the year. My May 18 anniversary comes so close to Mother's Day and my June 3 birthday that my gift receiving events are all in a wad. I should have planned it so that with Christmas and Valentine's Day, I could get a steady trickle of presents throughout the year.

Sounds silly, doesn't it? Oh, ladies! With God, it's not a steady trickle, but an ongoing, daily outpouring of the gifts of His mercy and grace. *"His compassions fail not. They are new every morning: great is thy faithfulness"* (Lamentations 3:22-23).

It's Christmastime, birthday, anniversary, Mother's Day, and Valentine's Day all wrapped up into *each* day! Let's start opening and see what is *in His presents!*

The Presents of Our Positions in Christ

Noah has always been a great help to me. Noah Webster that is. As I began thinking about how we can be more consciously aware of dwelling in God's presence by studying His presents to us, I thought I would see just what *presence* meant. The dictionary defines *presence* as being in "the neighborhood of one of superior [or] royal rank."[1] I remember an occasion several years ago when Arkansas Governor Bill Clinton came to our town to speak for our chamber of commerce banquet. I was to sing and someone asked if I was nervous performing before our head of state. I had to admit I was until I realized that on a regular basis I had the privilege of singing before the Creator of the universe, the great I AM, Jehovah God. Nothing could compare to that privilege!

How often we get our priorities confused. We bow and scrape, primp and prune if we think someone of *importance* might come our way and grace us with his presence. Yet our omnipotent Father invites us into His throne room. He longs to have us turn to Him, depend on Him, and visit with Him, and we are just not sure we can work Him into our schedule. Father, forgive us. We know not what we do.

God has given us a position in Christ, and yet we barely scratch the surface of all that is available to us through Him. Have you ever stopped just to dwell on all of the different ways we, as children of God, are identified in His Word?

First Peter 2:9 tells us, *"But ye are a chosen generation, a royal priesthood, an holy nation, a peculiar people; that ye should shew forth the praises of him who hath called you out of darkness into his marvellous light."* Let's look at each title more closely.

A Chosen Generation

Chosen: selected, picked. Each of us has experienced it. You remember those good ol' elementary days when the teacher appointed two captains for the kickball teams and then it began. The captains began choosing sides. Every child dreads being the last one picked. But if you are a child of God, if you have felt the burden and sorrow of your sin, if you have repented of that sin and turned to Jesus as your Savior, then you can remember being picked, selected, *chosen* by God to live in His presence.

Maybe it is best compared to being chosen by your mate. He pursued you, wooed you, chased you until he finally caught you and claimed you for his own. Why? He did it because he loved you. That's what God did with us. The scripture in 1 Peter is almost identical to Deuteronomy 7:6-8 where Moses tells Israel, *"the LORD thy God hath **chosen** thee to be a special people unto himself, above all people that are upon the face of the earth. The LORD did not set his love upon you, nor **choose** you, because ye were more in number than any people;... but because the LORD loved you."* (author's emphasis).

There it is plain and simple. It is not because we are worthy. It is not because we are lovable. It is not because we are mighty in number or deserving in deed. It is simply because He *chose* to love us. What a position! What a present!

A Royal Priesthood

We don't have a monarchy in the United States, but it seems that we are all drawn to news of the British royalty whenever it appears in our papers. Whether it was Lady Diana and Prince Charles, Fergie and Andrew, or now Prince William, we read and watch with interest as they make their every move. But why should we be so enamored with them when in fact we are royalty as well!

The Bible scholar Spiros Zodhiates defines the *royal priesthood* as, "belonging to, appointed, suitable for the king; a priesthood called to royal dominion or clothed with royal dignity."[2]

We belong to the King. That means we have a kingly ancestry. Not only are we related to Him, but also we are His subjects, appointed to be in service to the crown. We belong by birth. We are clothed in the royal dignity of His righteousness by His blood, and therefore, we are our own priest. No earthly man need go before the King in our behalf. We can, on our own, *"come boldly unto the throne of grace"* (Hebrews 4:16).

Why does He give us this special position and this wonderful present? So that we might *"offer up spiritual sacrifices, acceptable to God by Jesus Christ"* (1 Peter 2:5). What sacrifice does He want? Us! *"I beseech you therefore, brethren, by the mercies of God, that ye present your bodies a living sacrifice, holy, acceptable unto God, which is your reasonable service"* (Romans 12:1).

We are the offerer. We are the offering. We received this gift of royalty from God so that we, as our own priest, may give it back to Him.

A Holy Nation

To be holy means to be separated, set apart, sanctified, consecrated, chaste, and pure. That is an undertaking we are powerless to bring about without the presence of God in our lives. Zodhiates states it this way, "Its fundamental ideas are separation, consecration, devotion to God, and sharing in God's purity and abstaining from earth's defilement."[3]

Our part in attaining holiness is devoting ourselves to God. He sanctifies us and separates us from the world and to Himself. We cannot turn to Him unless He draws us.

Now, look at this. This word for *"nation"* used in 1 Peter 2:9 is *ethnos*. It frequently refers to the heathen or to Gentiles, distinguishing them from the Jews.[4] We are the heathen. We are the Gentiles. Yet God in His great mercy has given us the opportunity to accept the sacrifice of His Son and become holy unto Him, *"whether we be Jews or Gentiles, whether we be bond or free"* (1 Corinthians 12:13). What a position! What a present!

A Peculiar People

Come on; admit it! We are all guilty of making an observation about someone and declaring them a bit *peculiar*. And yet here I am saying what a wonderful position and glorious present it is for us to be considered peculiar!

When we think of *peculiar*, we think "odd, strange, weird." But Noah (remember that's Webster) may shed a little light on this subject. According to him, the definition includes shades of meaning that bring to light exactly what this scripture is saying. The word *peculiar* can also imply "being distinctive, belonging exclusively to one person, being considered special or different from the normal, private property."[5]

Isn't that great! There is a big POSTED sign written

across our lives. "Keep out, Satan. This one belongs to me. She is my private property and there will be no trespassing."

What safety and security, what peace and comfort, what joy and contentment to know we are special and exclusively God's property!

Other Positions

That's not all. There are other scriptures that indicate the fullness of the relationship we enjoy in Christ.

We are the sheep of His pasture. *"So we thy people and sheep of thy pasture will give thee thanks for ever: we will shew forth thy praise to all generations"* (Psalm 79:13). Sheep are dirty, dumb, and helpless creatures. But that's not the important part. Look whose pasture we, as God's sheep, are in — His! The ultimate shepherd wants to clothe, feed, and care for us. How silly of a sheep to say, "Thanks, but no thanks!" Instead, we should enjoy all that is ours in our position as His sheep.

We are soldiers of Jesus Christ. *"Thou therefore endure hardness, as a good soldier of Jesus Christ. No man that warreth entangleth himself with the affairs of this life; that he may please him who hath chosen him to be a soldier"* (2 Timothy 2:3-4). The battle is difficult and ongoing. The enemy is formidable and strong, but our Commander-in-Chief is stronger (1 John 4:4), and He has equipped us for battle (Ephesians 6:13-18).

We are heirs of God. Romans 8:17 calls us heirs of God and joint heirs with Christ. Umm, let's see. An heir usually inherits her father's goods. What does that entail with God as our Father? According to Psalms 104:24; 112:3; and 50:10 the earth is full of His riches and every beast in the forest and cattle on a thousand hills belongs to Him. That sounds like a pretty spiffy inheritance to me!

We Are His Children

Being chosen, how special. Being holy, how challenging. Being royal, how exciting. Being peculiar, how unique. Being sheep, how humbling. Being soldiers, how motivating. Being heirs, how blessed. But no title, no reference, no designation is more precious to me than the one given in Romans 8:16 that states, *"The Spirit itself beareth witness with our spirit, that we are the children of God."*

His Child. *His* child. His *child.* Think of your own children. Oh how we love them. We don't love everything they do, but we love them. They are part of us. Our blood runs through their veins. That nose, those eyes, and that mouth came from you or from their dad.

We pray for them, plan for them, dream for them, and have goals for them. If we truly love them, we submit them to God to be used always and only in His service, and we dedicate ourselves to that very purpose.

If we love our children this way, how much more does He love us? Our love is imperfect; His is perfect. Our love is fleeting; His is everlasting. Our love is sometimes parceled out depending upon the actions of the recipient. His love was given to us, not because we deserve it, but in spite of the fact that we don't!

We are part of Him. The blood of His Son flows through our spiritual veins and brings us close to the Father (Ephesians 2:13). He has plans, dreams, and goals for each of us (Jeremiah 29:11).

Can you begin to sense it? Can you feel the heart of the Father? Can you realize the love that you have for your own flesh and blood and comprehend that His love for us is infinitely greater and vastly deeper than we can fathom much less emulate?

"If ye then, being evil, know how to give good gifts unto your children, how much more shall your Father which is in heaven give good things to them that ask him?" (Matthew 7:11). So we ask for those good things

and in turn, He is *"able to do exceeding abundantly above all that we ask or think"* (Ephesians 3:20).

He gives gifts. He gives good gifts. He gives abundant gifts. And *in His presents*, He equips us for His work Why?

As a chosen generation, a royal priesthood, a holy nation, and a peculiar people *"that ye should shew forth the praises of him who hath called you out of darkness into his marvellous light"* (1 Peter 2:9).

As the sheep of his pasture that *"we will shew forth thy praise to all generations"* (Psalm 79:13).

As a soldier of Christ *"that he may please him who hath chosen him to be a soldier"* (2 Timothy 2:4).

As an heir of God that we should *"suffer with him, that we may be also glorified together"* (Romans 8:17.)

Do you remember the picture of John-John playing under the desk in the Oval Office while President Kennedy was on the phone? Here was the most powerful man in the world allowing his son to come play at his feet while he ran the country.

Oh, ladies! The omniscient, omnipotent, omnipresent God who takes care of every detail, of every aspect, of every thing in the universe not only allows it but longs for us to come into His throne room and be at His feet. You are His child. Come to your Father. Bow in humility before His throne. Fall prostrate before Him in your heart, your mind, and with your body. Begin to seek His presence as never before on a moment-by-moment basis. As you do, He will make known to you all of the wonderful, fathomless riches that are yours to enjoy in His presence *and* in His presents!

Unwrapping the Gifts

1. The greatest Gift of all that God has ever given is His Son, Jesus Christ. This study will be meaningless to you if you have not accepted Him as your Savior. If you

have never acknowledged your sinfulness before God, and if you have never admitted that you can only have a relationship with Him based on the precious blood of Jesus Christ, will you pray now and ask God to forgive you of your sins? Ask Jesus to be your Savior and Lord and to *"cleanse* [you] *from all unrighteousness"* (1 John 1:9). If you are taking this step now, write your prayer of repentance here, date it, and sign it.

_____

_____

2. If you are a child of God and have accepted the gift of His Son, take a few moments to record your experience then write a prayer of praise for your salvation.

_____

_____

3. Of all of the positions in Christ mentioned in this lesson, which is the most meaningful to you and why?

_____

_____

Which is the most challenging to you and why?

_____

_____

4. What hinders you from being in His presence at this time in your life?

Look over what you have just written and realize there are no reasons, only excuses!

5. What work must you allow God to do in you so that nothing comes between you and a closer relationship to the Father?

1. Noah Webster, *Webster's Seventh New Collegiate Dictionary* (Springfield, Massachusetts: G. & C. Merriam Company, 1965), 672.

2. Spiros Zodhiates, *The Complete Word Study New Testament* (Chattanooga, Tennessee: AMG Publishing, 1992), 896.

3. Ibid., 879.

4. Ibid., 908.

5. Webster, 621.

In His Presents

To the Present

Isn't the English language wonderful? I've been told that our language is one of the most difficult to learn. So many English words sound alike but have different meanings. Other words are spelled the same but pronounced differently and have different meanings. That's the way it is with the word *present.*

One definition of present covers the main thrust of this book. It is a gift. When you put the accent on the second syllable, it means to offer a gift or point of view. Still another rendering of the word deals with a time frame, the here and now.[1] It is this third interpretation that I want us to examine more closely.

I hope we are now more vibrantly attuned to the fact that we are in God's presence each and every moment of each and every day. We should vastly appreciate the positions He has given us that make being in His presence possible. But before we look forward to examine all that concept means for us and how it should shape our lives, let's take the time to look backward and see how God has always worked and moved in our lives to bring us to the present.

God has led us over mountains, around obstacles, and through valleys. He has protected us from Satan, human threats, and even ourselves. He has orchestrated events, situations, and circumstances in our lives to bring about His plans, His purposes, and His will. Perhaps you have never stopped to think back over your life and realize just how much God was involved. Maybe you've never examined the so-called happenstances to see that not only was He there, but also He was working all things to your good (Romans 8:28).

Look at Deuteronomy 26:1-11. In this account, Moses instructs the children of Israel to gather a basket of blessings. This was to be done when they came into the land which God had chosen for them and given to them. Five times in this passage he reminds them that it is the Lord Who had brought them to where they were. When the time came for them to enter the Promised Land, they were to first gather their offerings and bring them to the priest. Before the offerings were placed on the altar, the Israelites were to recount all that God had done for them.

Why would God want the people to go back over all the hardships and blessings of their pilgrimage? I think there are two reasons. First, He wanted them to remember His provisions for them. When they were ready to perish, He was there. When the Egyptians *"evil entreated* [them], *and afflicted* [them], *and laid upon* [them] *hard bondage,"* He was there (Deuteronomy 26:6).

Second, God wanted them to realize that since He had supplied their needs throughout all of the hardships of their past, they could now trust Him with their future. Who would have thought that their bondage and servitude was orchestrated by God? But it was! Since He was there to bring them through the wilderness and to the Promised Land, could they not now be assured that He would be there as they continued their journey and went in to possess the Promised Land? It wouldn't be easy. There would be battles. They would have to fight for what was promised to them by God, but He would be there with them! *"Be strong and of a good courage; be not afraid, neither be thou dismayed: for the LORD thy God is with thee whithersoever thou goest"* (Joshua 1:9).

Let's do the same thing! Before we open the gifts God has given us, and before we present those gifts as a basket of blessings back to the Lord, let's take a look back at all He has brought us through.

The only life I have lived is mine! I know that is a profound statement, but the only way I can show you what I want you to realize about God's presence in our lives is to share with you how I can look back and see how He has been with me every step of the way. While I'm looking back at my life, I want you to look back at yours.

This may truly be difficult. We have all had hurts and heartaches. We have all experienced fears and failures. We have all had our share of disappointments and denials. Whatever the situation, we must realize three things: (1) God's hand has constantly been on our lives; (2) nothing has happened to us without His knowledge; and (3) all events and circumstances were first sifted through His hands.

As I take you down memory lane and share with you the people, places, and events that have shaped my life, I want you to jot down the people, places, and events that have affected you. Some of these will be positive memories, and others will be negative. All of them have brought you to where you are today and are part of the process that God is using to mold you into what He wants you to be.

Age 0

Let's begin at conception. Frankly, I don't remember that part of my life, but God does! He not only remembers it, but He was right there selecting the exact sperm and the exact egg to make me me. This was no small task! He had millions of sperm to choose from and hundreds of eggs and each one had its own genetic code. There were trillions of possibilities and combinations, but it was no problem for Him. You see, He had it all planned out from eternity past. My parents received their genetic code from their parents, who received it from their parents and on it goes. In each and every conception of each and every child through each and every generation, God picked out every gene on every chromosome!

Let me show you what I mean. I never knew my paternal grandfather, John David Bates. He died when my daddy was only fifteen. I do know two things about him, though. Everyone who knew him said he was a good man, and he taught singing school. The first fact affected my life because he reared my daddy and instilled in him the essence of being a godly man. The second is important to me because I feel my love of music and singing must have come from my Grandpa Bates.

Grandmother Bates was a petite lady. I definitely did not get that gene! But Exa Beulah (Thankfully I wasn't named for her!) was a strict disciplinarian. My son, Jared, would say I got a double dose of that. It is what he calls "that mean Bates woman streak!" I'm sure he is teasing!

Then there was Papa, Dr. J. E. Cobb. He was wise and reflective, calm and mild. So far there is not much I can relate to. But, he loved studying and teaching and I do too. In fact, Papa was a school teacher, so I think I got my school teaching gene from him.

Granny Cobb's genetic code must have been strong on the genes God selected for me because she was my kind of woman. Matilda Elizabeth was fun and jolly. She loved people, and she loved to talk. For those who know me, need I say more?

That brings us to Daddy and Mama, Doyle and Bernice Bates. Most people say I look more like Mama

and act more like Daddy. I have her straightforward-
ness, but I didn't get her cleaning gene. (God used that
all up on my sister Jenny before He got to me.) I inher-
ited Daddy's temperament (and temper), his drive, his
people orientation, and his propensity to wrinkle
around the eyes, very prematurely I might add.

But there I am. From John and Beulah, Jesse and
Tildy, through Doyle and Bernice to Judy Lynn. Hand-
picked by God, special ordered, and made to specifications. There is no room for pride, I had nothing to do
with it. There is great cause for praise because if He
was so intimately involved with my conception, He
must really love me. He does! He really loves you too!

Unwrapping the Gifts

Read and meditate on Psalm 139. Jot down facts and
features of your grandparents and parents that you can
definitely see as being part of you. Praise Him that you
are so fearfully and wonderfully made.

Preschool

The next thing that I don't remember was when I was
five months old. That is when the doctor put me on my
first (of many) diet. Next to a picture of me taking a
bottle in my photo album, Mama had this comment,
"Judy eating; she liked to eat and she liked lots of it!"
Mama told me I would take sixteen ounces at a feeding.
For some reason the doctors thought that was too
much, and they put me on soy milk. Now see what a
sense of humor God has. At age five months, He had
me supporting the market of my future husband

Tommy who would grow up to be a soybean farmer.

Some of the first things I do remember were my experiences in day care. In Memphis, the lady who kept me was mean. I honestly don't remember her ever doing anything to hurt me physically, but I do remember her being cruel to some of the others. I also remember telling on her to the parents who would come and pick up their children. On the other hand, in Jackson, Tennessee, I went to a church day care and loved Mrs. "Chili" and Mrs. Brownie. Their real names were Mrs. Shelly and Mrs. Brownie Sandlin, but I always related everything to food.

My earliest church memories revolved around two special people, Howard Wells and Patsy Campbell from Temple Baptist Church in Little Rock, Arkansas. Brother Howard always led the children's department singing. He was tall and lanky and would use every bit of his frame to teach us our songs. He would wave his arms, go down on one knee, and get more music out of little people than anyone thought possible. I truly believe it was Brother Howard who gave me the confidence and desire to sing in front of people from the time I was three. I even remember one time when we were visiting a church for the first time and without my parents' knowledge I informed the Sunday School teacher I wanted to sing for the services, and so I did!

Patsy was my Sunday School teacher when I was three. I can still remember the Bible story of the four friends who brought the lame man to Jesus and lowered him through the roof. We *walked* up to the roof of the shoe box house with our fingers and let the tiny doll figure down by unrolling the string he was attached to. All the time and effort she took in preparing those lessons made a lasting impression on me.

Then there was Catherine. She was a three-hundred-pound African-American lady who kept me the year before I started to school. I loved every inch of her. She defended me against neighborhood bullies and tried to put me in her lap when I was afraid of thunderstorms. I don't remember Mama crying when I started to school, but Catherine did. Through her, God taught me, "red and yellow, black and white, they are precious in His sight."

Unwrapping the Gifts

Record any people, places, or events from your preschool years that shaped your life.

_____

_____

Elementary School

I could not wait to go to school. I wanted to read and write. I wanted to be around all of those other kids and organize all of the recesses for everyone. I simply wanted to learn. That love for school never diminished. In fact, it was in the third grade that God implanted in my heart the desire to be a teacher. I remember thinking, "I love school so much, I want to do something so that I can be in school always. I think I'll teach." The reason I know that direction was from God was that I never wavered from that goal. My parents tried to discourage me from teaching. They wanted me to be a dental hygienist. But from that day onward, I knew I should teach.

There are many other elementary memories. My favorite was the school Christmas party during my first grade year. We drew names, and it *just so happened* that I got the name of the girl in class that nobody wanted. She had raggedy, torn clothes; shoes that were much too big; yellow teeth; and an offensive body odor. I had no interest in picking out her gift and left it instead to Mama and Daddy. On the day of the party, most of the children exchanged the usual toys, books, perfumes, and fake jewelry. I couldn't tell you what I received, but I can tell you that I learned the true meaning of Christmas that year. My daddy had specifically asked the teacher for this child's name so that when she opened her gift, she found a new, warm coat. It was probably the first she had ever had. By his actions, my daddy showed me what the gift of a loving father can mean in the lives of so many people. My heavenly Father teaches me that, too.

Then in the third grade, I had my first boyfriend! That might not seem like such a big thing, but for me it was. You see, I was still battling a weight problem. At age eight, the doctors had put me on diet pills. I was in chubby sizes. In fact, I went straight from chubbies to misses with very few stops in the junior sizes. But Alfred still liked me. He liked me just the way I was. I didn't have to lose weight or do anything differently; he liked me! What an important lesson. God is like that. We don't have to clean up our act, change our appearance, jump through hoops, or anything. He loves us just the way we are.

March 10, 1960, was the most important day of my life. During a family devotional Mama was having while Daddy was out of town, I accepted Christ as my Savior. In the living room, in front of our red couch at 415 Willow Street, North Little Rock, Arkansas, I accepted His invitation to become His child. I've wandered from time to time, but He has never failed me yet. And do you know what? He never will.

My leadership abilities (some may refer to it as bossiness) began to emerge during my later elementary years. I started a cheerleading squad even when we had no team for which to cheer. I thought we needed cheerleaders anyway, and I got to decide who could and could not be on the squad. Of course, I was the captain. I also organized a debate every recess in the fifth grade between the Nixon and Kennedy supporters. I didn't know why, but I knew my daddy didn't want Kennedy to be president, so I thought I would do my part to see that he was defeated. History has proven that my efforts were futile, but my powerful personality was definitely beginning to take shape.

Then came our big move. In February 1962, God moved us to Fort Smith. Daddy knew it was God's leading, and he followed even though his three females fought it every step of the way. We didn't want to leave Little Rock. We didn't want to leave Temple Baptist Church. Jenny and I didn't want to go from being around a large group of young people at church to being the *only* young people at church.

But, oh the growth God brought to my life through that move. As a sixth grader, I became church pianist. The kids at school were so friendly and accepting of me from day one. The Lord impressed me then and there to go out of my way to always make the new student welcome. This even carried over into my days as middle school principal, and even now, I feel the utmost priority should be given to the new people at church. On that very first day at my new school, God brought into my life a friend who now lives only thirteen miles away, and we still get together for lunch. Isn't it amazing how our Father truly does know best!

Unwrapping the Gifts

Record particular events from your elementary years that influenced who you are today.

_____

_____

_____

Junior High and High School

My senior school annual refers to me as "Miss Participation Plus." Translated, that means if there was a club, I would join it. If there was an office to be held, I would try to hold it. If there was something I could be in charge of, that's what I would do! After all, didn't people check the length of your list of school activities that went with your senior picture? Appearances. That was so important to me. But all the while I was trying to add to my list, God was trying to add to my *"faith virtue; and to virtue knowledge; and to knowledge temperance; and to temperance patience; and to patience godliness; and to godliness brotherly kindness; and to brotherly kindness charity"* (2 Peter 1:5-7).

For instance, all through junior high and high school I tried out for cheerleader. I never made it. It wasn't until years later that it dawned on me that God had orchestrated that. You see, if I had ever made cheerleader I truly think I would have destroyed my voice that God now allows me to use to sing His praise.

Then there was student government. I tried for student body president in junior high and was defeated by two votes. When it came time for me to select my course of study for high school, I had to choose between student council and girls chorus, two of my very favorite things. God had His hand on that decision as well. He knew I would have the opportunity to develop my voice at Central Baptist College (CBC), but by choosing to go with student government, He was allowing me to develop my public speaking. On a regular basis, I was called on by our principal to give speeches in front of our 2000-plus student body. Also, I was put in charge of our high school's homecoming activities and Teacher Appreciation Day for two years. I couldn't have had better opportunities to develop organizational skills. Both of these experiences would come into play in later years as a school teacher, principal, and a public speaker for women's conferences. Isn't He awesome? Without my help and sometimes even with me battling Him every step of the way, He was working all things to my good.

Unwrapping the Gifts

Were there courses you took, clubs to which you belonged, friendships you developed, opportunities you had (or missed out on) during junior or senior high years that you can now see helped to mold you into what God had in mind for your life today? Record them here.

_____

_____

College

Next came college. The choice had been made for me by my parents that I would attend CBC. I began attending what was then called Senior Day when I was nine years old. I was there for the groundbreaking of the first student center. Years later as a member of the board, I was there for the groundbreaking of the new student services complex.

I started college as an English major. I just knew I was an outstanding writer, and I enjoyed reading so I thought that would be a perfect field. On the first day of class we were assigned an essay and warned by the teacher that we would all make an F. *She doesn't know me*, I thought. *I have had some wonderful teachers and I know how to use a thesaurus!* Sure enough, my first essay came back to me with a huge, red F on it and the comment, "You need to get a thesaurus."

On the other hand, after my first biology test, Dr. Harold Cooper came to me and said, "Judy, you did really well on your first test. I think you're going to be a good science student."

Guess what I did? I went right over and changed my major! Oh, the power of encouraging words. That one statement changed the course of my career. What I didn't know was at that time there was an abundance of English teachers and a shortage of science teachers. But God knew. I never had a problem finding a job. God always opened up just the right position, at just the right school, at just the right time.

It was also at CBC that God sent me my mate for life. Much has been said about girls going to CBC for their *MRS.* degree. What better place to find a soul mate! Oh, Tommy Wallace wasn't what I thought I needed. But he is exactly what God knew I needed to complete me in every way. How I love him, and how thankful I am to God Almighty for orchestrating our courtship and marriage. God is the best matchmaker there is.

Now, ladies, that is the story of my life. Through it all there has been one, overriding theme. God was present, always. He was there to protect me from mean day care ladies and to bless me with sweet ones. He was present to inspire me with Howard Wells and Patsy Campbell and to lead me away from cheerleading and into student government. He was there to encourage me with Dr. Cooper and guard and keep me for Tommy Wallace. On and on it goes.

The same is true for you. *"The steps of a good man are ordered by the LORD: and he delighteth in his way. Though he fall, he shall not be utterly cast down: for the LORD upholdeth him with his hand"* (Psalm 37:23-24).

Hold out your hands cupped in front of you. Go ahead; do it now! Visualize these hands as being God's hands. Now imagine that you are right there, living your life in the middle of those hands. Suppose you fell down, or you turned around and went the completely wrong way. Oops! You stubbed your toe. But look! All of it happened right in the middle of God's hands. You are under His watchful eye. You are upheld by His hands. Take time to thank Him for bringing you to the present.

Unwrapping the Gifts — Board of Directors Activity

Colleges, universities, banks, hospitals, foundations, institutions, and corporations all have a board of directors. Who are these people and what do they do?

Usually the board sets policy. That means they are the ones who set forth the vision and direction for the organization. They oversee the goals of the group they represent and try to make sure that all runs smoothly.

In going over the history of your life, God has brought to mind many people who have influenced you along the way. If you could select ten of them to be on the board of directors for your life, who would you choose and why? Besides actual people, you may also choose biblical heroes, people from history, or contemporaries that you've never met.

Truly give this some thought. If the person is alive today, take the time to write them a note and let them know what they mean to you.

Board of Directors

1. _____   6. _____

2. _____   7. _____

3. _____   8. _____

4. _____   9. _____

5. _____   10. _____

Now for a different twist. If the people in your circle of acquaintances were given this same assignment, would you be on their board of directors? Why or why not? What changes would God have to make in your life for Him to be able to use you to influence others to this extent (1 Timothy 4:12-16)?

_____

_____

_____

1. Webster, 672.

3

Boxes and Bows

To me, the most difficult thing about gift giving is the wrapping. It seems that the boxes are either too large or too small, the paper is either too adult or too juvenile, and if the bows aren't prefabricated, then the present doesn't get one! At Christmastime I try my best to shop at places that will do the wrapping for me, or else I talk my daughter Jill into helping.

Thankfully, God is not like that. He takes as much care and attention with the boxes and bows as He does with the gift that is inside. Why? Because we are the boxes and bows! He delights in selecting every part of who we are and that includes our personalities!

I was first introduced to the concept of the personalities in the early eighties when Mrs. Pat Quesenbury included them in her study, *The Feminine Touch.* What an eye-opener that was! For the first time, I could see that my husband Tommy wasn't being slow and methodical to get on my nerves; that was his personality. Also, the people with whom I was experiencing the most conflict at that time were simply exhibiting their personality traits that just so happened to be identical to mine.

A Biblical Basis for the Personalities

As far as I know the word *personality* or *temperament* never occurs in the Bible. For that matter, neither do the words rapture or trinity, but I believe the Bible teaches both of these concepts, and I enjoy studying and thinking about them.

So, too, I think we can confidently learn about our basic temperaments from a study of God's Word. We can see the distinctions by studying:

The Personalities of the Patriarchs,

The Plurality of all Persons,

The Plea from the Psalmist, and

The Possibility for Peace.

The Personalities of the Patriarchs

Let's look at the lives of some of the most noted men in the Bible. When we think of these men, we automatically think of certain characteristics they displayed in their relationship to God and others.

For example, when you think of the apostle Peter, what comes to mind? Peter was always talking. He spoke when he should have listened. He bragged on his commitment to the Savior just hours before he denied Him. He often displayed *foot-in-mouth* syndrome.

What about Paul? He was driven both before his salvation in the persecution of Christians and after his salvation in bringing others to Christ. He was forceful and outspoken. He had a job to do, and he was going to do it, in jail or out, before rulers, or before the common man.

Then there was Moses. He was such a great leader but so full of self-doubt. He lacked confidence in being able to do the job God was calling him to do. For every revelation of God's will, he had an excuse for not doing it. But what a detail man he was! Only a certain type of person could be given such details as he was given for the building of the tabernacle, and not only remember them but carry them out to the last item.

Of course, there was Abraham. I call him the *whatever* type of personality. This was to his advantage when God gave His call. Abraham's attitude to the call of God, even at the cost of Isaac's life, was that of *Whatever You say, Lord — wherever You send.* It was not so good, though, when Sarah devised the brilliant idea of Abraham going in to Hagar to produce offspring. Abraham's personality type doesn't like conflict, so he agreed to *whatever.* We also see this aversion to conflict when he was willing to lie about Sarah being his wife and doing *whatever* it took to protect himself from Abimelech.

"Now all these things happened unto them for ensamples: and they are written for our admonition, upon whom the ends of the world are come" (1 Corinthians 10:11). God let us see these men and women of the Bible in both their strengths and weaknesses. If we only saw the good, how discouraging that would be for us. But God let us see their faults and failures as well so that we could see how He transformed their lives and used them as they were to accomplish His plans.

In Exodus 3:6, God told Moses, *"I am the God of thy father, the God of Abraham, the God of Isaac, and the God of Jacob."* What was the next logical step in that list? "Moses, I am also the God of YOU!" Ladies, put your name in that sequence. "I am the God of Abraham, the God of Isaac, the God of Jacob and the God of (*your name*)." Just as He took who they were and what they had, He can take us and use us for His honor and glory.

In the New Testament we read, *"Jesus Christ the same yesterday, and to day, and for ever"* (Hebrews 13:8). The same God is ready to work in and through us today as He did in the lives of those in the Scriptures. So we can learn about our own boxes and bows from studying the personalities of the patriarchs.

The Plurality of All Persons

Mark 12:30 tells us, *"And thou shalt love the Lord thy God with all thy heart, and with all thy soul, and with all thy mind, and with all thy strength: this is the first commandment."* Now according to this verse, we all have a heart, a soul, a mind, and individual physical endowments as denoted by the word *"strength."* Since we are all unique and different physically, does it not make sense that we would be unique and different in our hearts, souls, and minds as well?

We do not all think alike with our minds. We do not all respond alike with our hearts. We do not all set about to solve problems in the same way with our souls, the will and chooser of our being. Whatever the situation is, in all ways we are to *"acknowledge him, and he shall direct thy paths"* (Proverbs 3:6). Some of us, such as my son and me, have extroverted, outgoing ways. Some, such as my husband and daughter, have quieter, more introverted ways. Each of us is to acknowledge Him in *all* of our ways so He can direct us in the way He so desires.

As parents we are told, *"Train up a child in the way he should go: and when he is old, he will not depart from it"* (Proverbs 22:6). *"In the way he should go,"* doesn't just mean according to God's principles but according to each child's *bent*, tendencies, natural inclinations, and individual strengths. In other words, according to their own personality and temperament! If you are the parent of more than one child, you know what I mean. What works for one in the area of training and discipline, does not necessarily work for the other. Each has to be dealt with individually.

A Plea From the Psalmist

Look at Psalm 139:23-24. Here David is asking God to do four things:

"Search me,... and know my heart:
Try me, and know my thoughts:...
See if there be any wicked way in me,...
Lead me in the way everlasting."
Why is he asking the Lord to do this work? If we take
it at face value, does it even make sense? Doesn't God
already know us and our hearts? Doesn't He already
know our motives and thoughts? In fact, hasn't David
already stated that very thing in the first two verses of
that very same Psalm? *"Thou hast searched me, and
known me. Thou knowest my downsitting and mine up-
rising"* (verse 2). So why is this request in verses 23 and
24?

I think the answer lies in the last phrase of verse 24
which states, *"Lead me in the way everlasting."* What
David is saying is, "God, You know me inside and out.
Now show *me* who I really am. Show me my sins and
shortcomings. Show me my frailties and weaknesses.
Show me who I am in Your eyes, not so I can excuse
my behavior but so I can repent, be forgiven, turn it all
over to you, and be led in the right direction."

First and foremost, this study of the personalities is
to help us better understand ourselves. As David, we
must ask God to search us, know our hearts; try us,
and know our thoughts; reveal to us all the filth we
have on the inside that He needs to bring to the surface
and remove. But also, let Him show us our outward
actions, the *"wicked ways"* that we might be blind to
but that are actually blinding others to the truth of life
in Christ. We must realize we all have strengths and
recognize that they are God-given and never should be
a source of pride. We must also realize that we all have
weaknesses and must seek the Holy Spirit's cure for
tendencies that keep us from being usable to God.

Hebrews 12:1 tells us to *"lay aside ... the sin which
doth so easily beset us."* Each temperament has a "besetting" sin. For some it may be anger; for others it

might be worry, fear, or procrastination. Power over these sins is only possible through the saving knowledge of Jesus Christ and a dependence on Him each moment of every day. Whether it is our strengths or our weaknesses, both should point us to God so that He might lead us into the way everlasting!

The Possibility of Peace

"If it be possible, as much as lieth in you, live peaceably with all men" (Romans 12:18). This scripture tells us three things:

The *Result*, or goal, is to "Live peaceably with all men."

The *Responsibility* is for us to do all we can (*"as much as lieth in you,"*) to reach that goal,

The *Realization* is that it may not always be possible, but *"if it be possible,"* we need to try.

We cannot control the actions, feelings, behaviors, or responses of other people, but we can control our actions, feelings, behaviors, and responses toward them. Part of that *"as much as lieth in you"* involves trying our best to understand the other person's bent, or her personality. In other words, we must try to walk in her proverbial moccasins, or see things through her eyes.

The information learned from a study of the personalities can truly be helpful if used in the right way. First, it will help you understand who you are, so you can capitalize on your strengths and turn your weaknesses over to the Father. Secondly, it should help you understand others, accept them as they are, and respond to them according to their needs.

The Golden Rule of God's moral law is to "Do unto others as you would have them do unto you." The Platinum Rule of the Personalities is "Do unto others as *they would have you do* unto them."

Our goal is to walk in the Spirit (Galatians 5:16), to be led of the Spirit (Galatians 5:18), and to display the fruit of the Spirit (Galatians 5:22). We want to be so Spirit-filled that others have trouble recognizing our particular personality bent. Christ had the strength of all the personalities and the weaknesses of none. The more time we spend with Him, the more we'll become like Him!

Unwrapping the Gifts

1. Of the four Bible characters mentioned in this study (Peter, Paul, Abraham, and Moses), which do you relate to more and why? Base this on the personality traits mentioned.

_____

_____

2. There are two major reasons to study the temperaments, understanding yourself better and relating to others better. At this time in your life, which is most important to you and why?

_____

_____

3. Go back over all of the individual scriptures listed in this lesson. Ask the Lord to impress a particular one on your heart. Meditate on that passage this week and jot down any insights or lessons that you learned.

_____

_____

_____

4. List your besetting sins, those that seem to be recurring or that you consistently have to deal with. Match them against the fruit of the Spirit listed in Galatians 5:22-23. Now read and follow 1 John 1:9. Thank God for His mercy and forgiveness.

_____

_____

_____

4

The Present of Our Personality

Can you remember when you first started learning how to read? In the old days of Dick, Jane, Spot, and Puff, we were taught by phonics. We spent days and weeks learning the alphabet and the sound of each letter. Then came the blends and the rules for using them, not to mention all the exceptions to the rules! It was tedious, and it was time consuming. But those of us who learned this way had a solid foundation. When we saw something new and unfamiliar, we could sound it out. It all started with the ABCs. Learning the rudiments helped us branch out into bigger, more difficult words until eventually we could read and comprehend most anything.

The same is true of understanding ourselves and others. There are some basic ABCs that we can learn about the four major personalities, and then it will be easier to understand the different combinations and blends that make each of us uniquely who we are.

Have you ever noticed how different you are from your parents and siblings or from your own mate or children? Have you ever made the comment that you (or your children) must have been found under a cabbage leaf since the way you (or they) do things is so completely opposite to the way others would have them done?

Well then, welcome to Personalities 101. Maybe this basic course is just what you need to help you appreciate that person you sometimes don't even want to be around. It may even help you answer the question, "Now, why did I do that?"

This concept is not new. Hippocrates lived hundreds of years before Christ, yet he was one of the first to write about the personalities, or as he referred to them, the temperaments. (These two words will be used interchangeably throughout this study.) The word *temperament* comes from Latin and actually means the "right-blending." Hippocrates was referring to the blending of what was then considered the four basic body fluids — blood, phlegm, choler or yellow bile, and melancholy or black bile.

"It was thought that there were four types, or temperaments, depending upon which fluid predominated in any mixture: the *sanguine* (blood) being rich-blooded, warm, lively; the *melancholic* (from the Greek *melaina chole*, black bile), dark and gloomy; the *choleric* (from the Greek *chole*, yellow bile), hot-tempered and violent; and the *phlegmatic* (from the Greek *phlegma*, phlegm or mucus), cool, slow, and sluggish."[1]

Although the idea of the fluids has long been abandoned, the concept of four basic personalities is alive and well. It has been renamed and repackaged to fit the arena in which it is taught, but the foundational message remains the same.

In the educational realm, it has been taught as *True Colors* whereby the personalities are identified by the colors orange, gold, green, or blue. In the business world, there is *DISC* with each letter representing one of the four. In their home and family seminars, John Trent and Gary Smalley use animals (the otter, lion, beaver, and golden retriever) to convey the differences.

In some of my training sessions and speaking opportunities I have used the punctuation marks (exclamation point, period, question mark, and comma) to help people get a better grasp of these concepts. However, one of the most practical and easiest naming systems is the one used by Florence and Marita Littauer in their conferences and writings. They specify the personalities as:

The Popular Sanguine
The Powerful Choleric
The Perfect Melancholy
The Peaceful Phlegmatic.

Just by reading the adjectives before each personality, can't you already get a picture in your mind of the kind of person each describes?

It is really quite simple. Remember we must go back to our ABCs for a better understanding. The ABCs of personality refer to:

A — Appearance (both personal and work area);
B — Behavior (body language and aura);
C — Communication (frequency and tone).

Let's look more closely at these Ps in our personality pod and see if we can recognize ourselves and others. These will be given in the extreme. They are caricatures and since few people are 100 percent of one personality, you may not see all of the things mentioned or at least not to the excess that they are described. Simply look for the overall impression.

The Popular Sanguine

The Popular Sanguine is the fun personality. The ultimate goal for these people in life is to have fun and to have everyone think they are funny. Usually, you will hear these people before you see them. They are rather loud and boisterous and not just in their voice, but also in their looks. It is the popular personality that will dress for attention. The colors will be bright; the patterns will be bold; the hair, the outfit, and the accessories will scream, "Look at me!" They want to be the life of the party and the center of attention. Their story is always the best, and they can usually have a crowd gathered around them to hear the next anecdote.

Their body language is like their mouth — open! They make big gestures and grand entrances. It is usually said of Sanguines that if you tied their hands down they couldn't talk. They are very affectionate and enjoy hugging anyone and everyone. They are emotional people and the most apt to invade another's personal space.

As far as their work area is concerned, cluttered would be the definitive word. They are usually creative people, but they have trouble staying on task until the job is finished. They can always find something else to do that is more interesting than what they are working on at the time. They are great starters, they begin numerous projects and volunteer to help with all committees, but they're poor finishers. Let's just say perseverance isn't their strong point.

Communication? They love it as long as they are the ones doing the talking and it requires very little listening on their part.

If they were a Trent and Smalley animal, they would be the playful otter. In *True Colors*, they would be orange. And of course, the perfect punctuation mark for the Popular Sanguine would be the exclamation point!

The apostle Peter was a Sanguine. He was always talking. When he and John went to see the tomb after hearing that Jesus arose, he simply pushed John aside to go in and check for himself. He was the loudest to proclaim his allegiance to Christ. He was the first to jump forward and cut off the soldier's ear in the Garden. He was the only one to climb over the edge of the boat into the stormy waters. But he lacked the perseverance. He denied the Lord, and when the rooster crowed, he went out and wept bitterly.

Perhaps you live with a Popular Sanguine. My son Jared is predominantly this temperament. He definitely enjoys making people laugh and wants to constantly be the center of attention. His sister says he got out of many spankings by making me laugh. I say he made me laugh, but he still got the spankings!

One of my favorite stories about Jared shows his typical popular personality. One weekend Brother George Reddin was at our church promoting Lifeword. Our pastor, Brother Jerry Goodwin, was in the pulpit getting ready to introduce Brother George. The projector was ready for the presentation with the white light shining on the screen. While there was a lull in the activity, Jared began to make animal shapes with his hands on the screen right there in the middle of the service! What makes this so horrifying for his mother is that he was twenty-three at the time.

The Powerful Choleric

A look at the appearance, behavior, and communication styles of the choleric makes them easy to spot. Often the people with the Powerful personality will have stern looks on their faces. This does not necessarily mean they are angry; they are just extremely focused. They have a job to do, and they will do it, with or without you.

The choleric's main desire is control. They need to feel they are in charge of the situation because they are sure their way of doing something is, of course, the best way. While a Popular Sanguine might be going from point A to point B and get sidetracked on the way to the extent they forget where they were going and why, the Powerful Choleric goes directly from point A to point B. They never forget. Not only do they know where they are and why they are there, but so will everyone else. They will organize, synchronize, and delegate so that the task is done in the most efficient manner. Never mind that they've run roughshod over feelings in the process; the job will be completed.

They are very capable and professional people. The main criteria for their clothing is practicality and function. While a Sanguine's office may have piles, the Choleric has piles of files. They are working on many projects, but they are focused and organized in the way they carry them out.

Cholerics are also usually easy to detect as soon as they enter a room. It is not by their voice, but more so their walk. They have a heavy, determined, floor-shaking walk. Other body language that is a dead giveaway for this temperament is the gestures they use. They are usually pointing their finger in the air or in your face, pounding their fist on a table or their other hand, or standing with both hands on their hips with that how-could-you-be-so-stupid look on their face.

They exude confidence and can run and organize anything. Once they have taken care of one project, they will look for the next challenge. They thrive on change. According to *True Colors* they would be the gold. The animal that typifies this temperament is the lion, king of the jungle. Their punctuation mark is the period. They've said it; that's it. No discussion. PERIOD.

Paul was a Powerful Choleric. He didn't care who he was talking to or where he was. He had a job to do and he was going to do it. This was true both before and after his conversion. He would confront leaders and rulers or even his fellow believers if he disagreed. When Peter was wrong at the Jerusalem council, Paul didn't mind letting him know it. He would have none of Barnabas' idea to take John Mark with them a second time and even split company because of this difference of opinion. Later, we see how God mellowed him, and he admitted his love and appreciation for Mark.

I know this personality all too well because it is my

dominate one. I also have a good dose of Popular Sanguine as is evidenced by my love of talking and being up front. My main motivation is getting things done that need to be done and doing so in a timely manner. This temperament has been clear since early in my childhood when I organized the cheerleading squads and presidential debates of which I was always in charge!

The Perfect Melancholy

The opposite of the Popular Sanguine is the Perfect Melancholy. While the Sanguines are loud and open with their mouths and gestures, the Melancholies are quiet and subdued. The Sanguine feeds on the attention of other people, while the Melancholies would much rather work alone. Their voice is almost monotone and any gestures they might have are very small, precise, and close to their body.

Melancholies are perhaps the neatest of all the temperaments. Their closets are usually organized according to color and length. All of the short-sleeved blouses are together as are the long-sleeved, and they are placed according to color. The color is not too dramatic; however, they rarely venture away from the basics. It is not *if* they are going to wear khaki or navy today, but *which* khaki and navy they should wear. Check out their billfolds. All of the bills are placed facing the same direction according to denomination.

Perfect Melancholies are the least likely to show affection. They tend not to be huggers and will usually stiffen or cringe when the loving Sanguine heads for them with open arms. After all, the Popular Sanguine is invading their space and might wrinkle them.

In *True Colors*, the Melancholies would be the green. They are the analytical thinkers, the detail people that all organizations need. Do you remember the commercial when the young man is proposing to his girlfriend in a restaurant? She's not at all sure about this until he gets out the line graph and shows how his love for her has increased over the previous month. Then he whips out a Venn Diagram showing the possible combination of features for their children. On it goes until he grabs the attention of his Melancholy lady with all of his charts.

Trent and Smalley peg these folks as the beavers of society. Just leave them alone and allow them to finish their work. They are usually talented and creative and would be the question marks of society. They are always wanting to know the whys and wherefores, the ins and outs of all things.

Moses is our biblical example of the Melancholy. He was full of self-doubt. He could always come up with an excuse to God as to why he couldn't do something. But, oh what a detail man he was. Just think about it, ladies. After God gave Moses the rules and regulations for sacrifices and offerings, the details about every aspect of the tabernacle, Moses had the organized, detailed mind to carry out all of God's instructions. Only a Melancholy could do that.

Mama was a Perfect Melancholy. As I shared with you previously, I didn't get her cleaning gene, but when she and Daddy would come to our house for a visit, believe me we would get in the cleaning mode. Mama was one of those people with extremely organized closets and drawers. Even her undies were folded and stacked just so. I'll never forget that Jenny and I learned to iron by pressing our sheets for the bed and Daddy's handkerchiefs and boxer shorts. I don't know how comfortable it was for Daddy, but it made Mama happy.

The last time Mama was at my house before she died was when she came for Jill's high school graduation. We had done our thorough *Mimi cleaning*, or so we thought. Saturday morning I found her on my front porch, sweat dripping from her face as she jabbed at all of our dirt dauber's nests with the handle of a broom. Her comment to me when I walked out was, "You sure must love Tommy Wallace to put up with all of this mess!"

Let me see — Tommy/dirt daubers? Tommy/dirt daubers? Yeah, I guess he's worth it!

The Peaceful Phlegmatic

Last but not least are the Peaceful Phlegmatics. We usually discuss them last, not because they are least important, it is just that their characteristics are least obvious. The other three personalities usually have some extreme that is easily recognizable. The Sanguine is loud, funny, and the center of attention. The Choleric is focused, determined, and in control. The Melancholy is quiet, pensive, and detailed. Not the Phlegmatic! Their most apparent characteristic is that they are usually not noticeable. They are the calm, easy-going people that everyone loves. It is about the Phlegmatic person that people always make a comment as, "He is the nicest guy," or "She is the sweetest girl." Marita Littauer usually refers to them as the *beauty queen* personality. Think about it. A beauty queen usually has no one feature that draws people's attention, just the overall appearance of beauty. That's the Phlegmatic! No one characteristic stands out, just an overall sense of peace.

In some ways Phlegmatics are chameleons. They take on the characteristics of the other personalities when they need to. They are known for their wonderful, dry sense of humor and are often placed in positions of leadership because everyone likes them and they have few enemies.

Peaceful Phlegmatics adopt the motto, "Why stand when you can sit? Why sit when you can lie down?" They are big into comfort, and it shows in their work space and their clothing. Should you look up the term laid-back in the dictionary, I feel sure you would find a picture of a Phlegmatic right next to the definition.

According to *True Colors* the Phlegmatics would be blue. They are harmonious people and more than anything they avoid conflict. Remember, they are *peaceful.* They are the golden retriever in the Trent and Smalley classifications. The loyal, calm, friend who is always quietly by your side. As a punctuation mark the Phlegmatics would be a comma. Why? Because a comma indicates a pause in the sentence. Phlegmatics pause. (Sometimes for extended periods.)

Abraham was a classic phlegmatic. He wanted no conflicts; just keep the peace. Now his *whatever* response was admirable when it came to his reaction to God's call to move. But he carried it to extremes when dealing with people. God had promised him a son. Sarah, his impatient and powerful wife, thought she would help God out and suggested that her husband go in to Hagar and father a child with her. What did he say? "Whatever." (That's a loose translation.) When he went to Egypt and feared for his life, he came up with a scheme and did *whatever* it took to save himself, even if it meant putting Sarah in danger.

I am married to a Phlegmatic. Just as the Sanguine is opposite from the Melancholy, so the Phlegmatic is opposite to the Choleric. There goes God's sense of humor again. He put my dear, sweet, calm, Phlegmatic husband with a raving, fireball, Choleric wife.

My favorite Tommy example is very typical of Phlegmatics. It is the where-do-you-want-to-go-to-eat question or a similar one of equally unimportant consequence. The usual response (99 times out of 100) is, "I don't care. Where do you want to eat?" Those of you who are peaceful find nothing wrong with this. Those of us who are powerful just want you to make a decision. But then of course when you do it will probably not be the one we wanted you to make, so then we must put in our two-cents worth anyway. Sound familiar, ladies? Does anyone other than me go through this?

It took me *years* to realize that Tommy wasn't trying to irritate me by not making a decision as to where we would eat. He really didn't care. Imagine that.

How frustrated I would be if God had placed me with someone who had as similar temperament to mine. First, I never would have been able to talk as much as I like to. But most important, I never would have learned how beautiful it is to be truly complete with a husband who fills in for all of my weaknesses and has taught me, with the Lord's help, to tone down those obnoxious characteristics. Me, a powerful/popular blend submit to him, a peaceful/perfect blend? Yes, and by doing so we have a strong oneness that may not have been developed otherwise. God is the perfect matchmaker.

Unwrapping the Gift

1. As you read about the personalities, did you gain a better understanding of yourself or someone else? If so, what was it and how will it help you in the future?

_____

_____

2. Was it easier for you to identify yourself from the strengths or the weaknesses mentioned about the personalities? Why do you think that is true? Does that in itself tell you anything about your personality?

_____

_____

3. Spend some time this week studying the Biblical character that represents your personality. Jot down words, phrases, adjectives that would show the personality he had. Be prepared to share what you've learned from this examination.

Popular Peter — He is mentioned throughout the gospels and Acts. He wrote 1 and 2 Peter. Also check Galatians 1:18; 2:7-14.

Powerful Paul — Browse through Acts 7:58-28:31 and all of his New Testament letters.

Perfect Moses — His story is found from Exodus through Deuteronomy. Also check Acts 7:22-37 and Hebrews 11:23-29.

Peaceful Abraham — Check out Genesis 11-25; Acts 7:2-8; Romans 4; Galatians 3; Hebrews 2; 6-7; 11.

_____

_____

_____

1. O. Hallesby, *Temperament and the Christian Faith* (Minneapolis, Minnesota: Augsberg Publishing House, 1962) page 8.

Author's Note: I acknowledge my indebtedness to Florence and Marita Littauer for their teaching and training on the personalities. Many of my ideas and examples came from their seminars and books.

Florence Littauer. *Personality Plus* (Grand Rapids, Michigan: Fleming H. Revell, 1992).

Florence and Marita Littauer. *Personality Puzzle* (Grand Rapids, Michigan: Fleming H. Revell, 1992).

Florence and Marita Littauer. *Personality Tree* (Dallas, Texas: Word Publishing, 1986).

Florence and Marita Littauer. *Getting Along With Almost Anybody, The Complete Personality Book* (Grand Rapids, Michigan: Fleming H. Revell, 1998).

5

What's in My Box

Christmas is always a big deal in our family. I'm sure it is in yours too. We always went to Mama and Daddy's in Fort Smith for the holidays. At their house would be my sister Jenny, her husband Gary, and their children Warren, David, and Melissa. Of course Tommy, Jared, Jill, and I would be there as well. Three families' gifts were all piled around one tree in their den.

Opening time was a big production. We always had a circle prayer before we began tearing into the boxes, and then Daddy would play Santa. He would heap the gifts beside each person until they had all been distributed. The only problem was, everyone was so busy opening their gifts, we never got to enjoy watching others open theirs.

Mama decided there must be a better way. So for the last few years, we began to open the gifts one person at a time. Each person would open a gift while everyone else watched. It took twice as long, but that way we were able to enjoy what everyone received.

You know what that must have been like. Oh, sure, you oohed and aahed at just the right times, but you were ready for it to be your turn so you could find out what was in your box.

Well, ladies, it's your turn. It's time for you to look inside this personality box that God has given you and see just what is inside. You may already have a pretty good idea after reading the last chapter, but let's examine ourselves in more detail.

The following personality profile developed by Fred Littauer will help you more accurately determine your dominant temperament. Get your pencil, have fun, be honest, and get ready to learn all about you.

Your Personality Profile

In each of the following rows of four words across, place an X in front of the one or two words that most often applies to you. Continue through all forty lines. If you are not sure which word most applies, ask a spouse or a friend, and think of what your answer would have been when you were a child. Use the word definitions following the profile for the most accurate results.

Strengths

1	Adventurous	Adaptable	Animated	Analytical
2	Persistent	Playful	Persuasive	Peaceful
3	Submissive	Self-sacrificing	Sociable	Strong-willed
4	Considerate	Controlled	Competitive	Convincing
5	Refreshing	Respectful	Reserved	Resourceful
6	Satisfied	Sensitive	Self-reliant	Spirited
7	Planner	Patient	Positive	Promoter
8	Sure	Spontaneous	Scheduled	Shy
9	Orderly	Obliging	Outspoken	Optimistic
10	Friendly	Faithful	Funny	Forceful
11	Daring	Delightful	Diplomatic	Detailed
12	Cheerful	Consistent	Cultured	Confident
13	Idealistic	Independent	Inoffensive	Inspiring
14	Demonstrative	Decisive	Dry humor	Deep
15	Mediator	Musical	Mover	Mixes easily

16	Thoughtful	Tenacious	Talker	Tolerant
17	Listener	Loyal	Leader	Lively
18	Contented	Chief	Chartmaker	Cute
19	Perfectionist	Pleasant	Productive	Popular
20	Bouncy	Bold	Behaved	Balanced

Weaknesses

21	Blank	Bashful	Brassy	Bossy
22	Undisciplined	Unsympathetic	Unenthusiastic	Unforgiving
23	Reticent	Resentful	Resistant	Repetitious
24	Fussy	Fearful	Forgetful	Frank
25	Impatient	Insecure	Indecisive	Interrupts
26	Unpopular	Uninvolved	Unpredictable	Unaffectionate
27	Headstrong	Haphazard	Hard to please	Hesitant
28	Plain	Pessimistic	Proud	Permissive
29	Angered easily	Aimless	Argumentative	Alienated
30	Naive	Negative attitude	Nervy	Nonchalant
31	Worrier	Withdrawn	Workaholic	Wants credit
32	Too sensitive	Tactless	Timid	Talkative
33	Doubtful	Disorganized	Domineering	Depressed
34	Inconsistent	Introvert	Intolerant	Indifferent
35	Messy	Moody	Mumbles	Manipulative
36	Slow	Stubborn	Show-off	Skeptical
37	Loner	Lord over others	Lazy	Loud
38	Sluggish	Suspicious	Short-tempered	Scatter-brained
39	Revengeful	Restless	Reluctant	Rash
40	Compromising	Critical	Crafty	Changeable

Strengths

1 **Adventurous.** One who will take on new and daring enterprises with a determination to master them.

Adaptable. Easily fits and is comfortable in any situation.

Animated. Full of life, lively use of hand, arm, and face gestures.

Analytical. Likes to examine the parts for their logical and proper relationships.

2 **Persistent.** Sees one project through to its completion before starting another.

Playful. Full of fun and good humor.

Persuasive. Convinces through logic and fact rather than charm or power.

Peaceful. Seems undisturbed and tranquil and retreats from any form of strife.

3 **Submissive.** Easily accepts any other's point of view or desire with little need to assert her own opinion.

Self-sacrificing. Willingly gives up her own personal being for the sake of, or to meet the needs of others.

Sociable. One who sees being with others as an opportunity to be cute and entertaining rather than as a challenge or business opportunity.

Strong-willed. Determined to have one's own way.

4 **Considerate.** Having regard for the needs and feelings of others.

Controlled. Has emotional feelings but rarely displays them.

Competitive. Turns every situation, happening, or game into a contest and always plays to win.

Convincing. Can win you over to anything through the sheer charm of his personality.

5 **Refreshing.** Renews and stimulates or makes others feel good.

Respectful. Treats others with deference, honor, and esteem.

Reserved. Self-restrained in expression of emotion or enthusiasm.

Resourceful. Able to act quickly and effectively in virtually all situations.

6 **Satisfied.** A person who easily accepts any circumstance or situation.

Sensitive. Intensively cares about others, and what happens.

Self-reliant. An independent person who can fully rely on her own capabilities, judgment, and resources.

Spirited. Full of life and excitement.

7 **Planner.** Prefers to work out a detailed arrangement beforehand, for the accomplishment of project or goal, and prefers involvement with the planning stages and the finished product rather than the carrying out of the task.

Patient. Unmoved by delay, remains calm and tolerant.

Positive. Knows it will turn out right if she's in charge.

Promoter. Urges or compels others to go along, join, or invest through the charm of her own personality.

8 **Sure.** Confident, rarely hesitates or wavers.

Spontaneous. Prefers all of life to be impulsive, unpremeditated activity, not restricted by plans.

Scheduled. Makes, and lives according to, a daily plan, dislikes her plan to be interrupted.

Shy. Quiet, doesn't easily instigate a conversation.

9 **Orderly.** Having a methodical, systematic arrangement of things.

Obliging. Accommodating. One who is quick to do it another's way.

Outspoken. Speaks frankly and without reserve.

Optimistic. Sunny disposition who convinces self and others that everything will turn out all right.

10 **Friendly.** A responder rather than an initiator, seldom starts a conversation.

Faithful. Consistently reliable, steadfast, loyal, and devoted sometimes beyond reason.

Funny. Sparkling sense of humor that can make virtually any story into a hilarious event.

Forceful. A commanding personality whom others would hesitate to take a stand against.

11 **Daring.** Willing to take risks; fearless, bold.

Delightful. A person who is upbeat and fun to be with.

Diplomatic. Deals with people tactfully, sensitively, and patiently.

Detailed. Does everything in proper order with a clear memory of all the things that happen.

12 **Cheerful.** Consistently in good spirits and promoting happiness in others.

Consistent. Stays emotionally on an even keel, responding as one might expect.

Cultured. One whose interests involve both intellectual and artistic pursuits, such as theatre, symphony, ballet.

Confident. Self-assured and certain of own ability and success.

13 **Idealistic.** Visualizes things in their perfect form, and has a need to measure up to that standard herself.

Independent. Self-sufficient, self-supporting, self-confident and seems to have little need of help.

Inoffensive. A person who never says or causes anything unpleasant or objectionable.

Inspiring. Encourages others to work, join, or be involved, and makes the whole thing fun.

14 **Demonstrative.** Openly expresses emotion, especially affection, and doesn't hesitate to touch others while speaking to them.

Decisive. A person with quick, conclusive, judgment-making ability.

Dry humor. Exhibits *dry* wit, usually one-liners which can be sarcastic in nature.

Deep. Intense and often introspective with a distaste for surface conversation and pursuits.

15 **Mediator.** Consistently finds herself in the role of

reconciling differences in order to avoid conflict.

Musical. Participates in or has a deep appreciation for music, is committed to music as an art form, rather than the fun of performance.

Mover. Driven by a need to be productive, is a leader whom others follow, finds it difficult to sit still.

Mixes easily. Loves a party and can't wait to meet everyone in the room, never meets a stranger.

16 **Thoughtful.** A considerate person who remembers special occasions and is quick to make a kind gesture.

Tenacious. Holds on firmly, stubbornly, and won't let go until the goal is accomplished.

Talker. Constantly talking, generally telling funny stories and entertaining everyone around, feeling the need to fill the silence in order to make others comfortable.

Tolerant. Easily accepts the thoughts and ways of others without the need to disagree with or change them.

17 **Listener.** Always seems willing to hear what you have to say.

Loyal. Faithful to a person, ideal, or job, sometimes beyond reason.

Leader. A natural born director, who is driven to be in charge, and often finds it difficult to believe that anyone else can do the job as well.

Lively. Full of life, vigorous, energetic.

18 **Contented.** Easily satisfied with what she has, rarely envious.

Chief. Commands leadership and expects people to follow.

Chartmaker. Organizes life, tasks, and problem solving by making lists, forms or graphs.

Cute. Precious, adorable, center of attention.

19 **Perfectionist.** Places high standards on herself,

and often on others, desiring that everything be in proper order at all times.

Pleasant. Easygoing, easy to be around, easy to talk with.

Productive. Must constantly be working or achieving, often finds it very difficult to rest.

Popular. Life of the party and therefore much desired as a party guest.

20 **Bouncy.** A bubbly, lively personality, full of energy.

Bold. Fearless, daring, forward, unafraid of risk.

Behaved. Consistently desires to conduct herself within the realm of what she feels is proper.

Balanced. Stable, middle of the road personality, not subject to sharp highs or lows.

Weaknesses

21 **Blank.** A person who shows little facial expression or emotion.

Bashful. Shrinks from getting attention, resulting from self-consciousness.

Brassy. Showy, flashy, comes on strong, too loud.

Bossy. Commanding, domineering, sometimes overbearing in adult relationships.

22 **Undisciplined.** A person whose lack of order permeates most every area of her life.

Unsympathetic. Finds it difficult to relate to the problems or hurts of others.

Unenthusiastic. Tends to not get excited, often feeling it won't work anyway.

Unforgiving. One who has difficulty forgiving or forgetting a hurt or injustice done to them; apt to hold onto a grudge.

23 **Reticent.** Unwilling or struggles against getting involved, especially when complex.

Resentful. Often holds ill feelings as a result of real or imagined offenses.

Resistant. Strives, works against, or hesitates to

accept any other way but her own.

Repetitious. Retells stories and incidents to entertain you without realizing she has already told the story several times before; is constantly needing something to say.

24 **Fussy.** Insistent over petty matters or details, calling for a great attention to trivial details.

Fearful. Often experiences feelings of deep concern, apprehension, or anxiousness.

Forgetful. Lack of memory which is usually tied to a lack of discipline and not bothering to mentally record things that aren't fun.

Frank. Straightforward, outspoken, and doesn't mind telling you exactly what she thinks.

25 **Impatient.** A person who finds it difficult to endure irritation or wait for others.

Insecure. One who is apprehensive or lacks confidence.

Indecisive. The person who finds it difficult to make any decision at all. (Not the personality that labors long over each decision in order to make the perfect one.)

Interrupts. A person who is more of a talker than a listener, who starts speaking without even realizing someone else is already speaking.

26 **Unpopular.** A person whose intensity and demand for perfection can push others away.

Uninvolved. Has no desire to listen or become interested in clubs, groups, activities, or other people's lives.

Unpredictable. May be ecstatic one moment and down the next, or willing to help but then disappears, or promises to come but forgets to show up.

Unaffectionate. Finds it difficult to verbally or physically demonstrate tenderness openly.

27 **Headstrong.** Insists on having his own way.

Haphazard. Has no consistent way of doing things.

Hard to please. A person whose standards are set so high that it is difficult to ever satisfy them.

Hesitant. Slow to get moving and hard to get involved.

28 **Plain.** A middle-of-the-road personality without highs or lows and showing little, if any, emotion.

Pessimistic. While hoping for the best, this person generally sees the down side of a situation first.

Proud. One with great self-esteem who sees herself as always right and the best person for the job.

Permissive. Allows others (including children) to do as they please in order to keep from being disliked.

29 **Angered easily.** One who has a childlike flash-in-the-pan temper that expresses itself in tantrum style and is over and forgotten almost instantly.

Aimless. Not a goal-setter with little desire to be one.

Argumentative. Incites arguments generally because she is right no matter what the situation may be.

Alienated. Easily feels estranged from others, often because of insecurity or fear that others don't really enjoy her company.

30 **Naive.** Simple and child-like perspective, lacking sophistication or comprehension of what the deeper levels of life are really about.

Negative attitude. One whose attitude is seldom positive and is often able to see only the down or dark side of each situation.

Nervy. Full of confidence, fortitude, and sheer guts, often in a negative sense.

Nonchalant. Easy-going, unconcerned, indifferent.

31 **Worrier.** Consistently feels uncertain, troubled, or anxious.

Withdrawn. A person who pulls back to herself and needs a great deal of alone or isolation time.

Workaholic. An aggressive goal-setter who must be constantly productive and feels very guilty when resting, is not driven by a need for perfection or completion but by a need for accomplishment and reward.

Wants credit. Thrives on the credit or approval of others. As an entertainer this person feeds on the applause, laughter, and/or acceptance of an audience.

32 **Too sensitive.** Overly introspective and easily offended when misunderstood.

Tactless. Sometimes expresses herself in a somewhat offensive and inconsiderate way.

Timid. Shrinks from difficult situations.

Talkative. An entertaining, compulsive talker who finds it difficult to listen.

33 **Doubtful.** Characterized by uncertainty and lack of confidence that it will ever work out.

Disorganized. Lack of ability to ever get life in order.

Domineering. Compulsively takes control of situations and/or people, usually telling others what to do.

Depressed. A person who feels down much of the time.

34 **Inconsistent.** Erratic, contradictory, with actions and emotions not based on logic.

Introvert. A person whose thoughts and interest are directed inward, lives within herself.

Intolerant. Appears unable to withstand or accept another's attitudes, point of view, or way of doing things.

Indifferent. A person to whom most things don't matter one way or the other.

35 **Messy.** Living in a state of disorder, unable to find things.

Moody. Doesn't get very high emotionally, but easily slips into low lows, often when feeling unappreciated.

Mumbles. Will talk quietly under the breath when pushed, doesn't bother to speak clearly.

Manipulative. Influences or manages shrewdly or deviously for her own advantage, will get her way somehow.

36 **Slow.** Doesn't often act or think quickly, too much of a bother.

Stubborn. Determined to exert her own will, not easily persuaded, obstinate.

Show-off. Needs to be the center of attention, wants to be watched.

Skeptical. Disbelieving, questioning the motive behind the words.

37 **Loner.** Requires a lot of private time and tends to avoid other people.

Lord over. Doesn't hesitate to let you know that she is right or is in control.

Lazy. Evaluates work or activity in terms of how much energy it will take.

Loud. A person whose laugh or voice can be heard above others in the room.

38 **Sluggish.** Slow to get started, needs push to be motivated.

Suspicious. Tends to suspect or distrust others or ideas.

Short-tempered. Has a demanding impatience-based anger and a short fuse. Anger is expressed when others are not moving fast enough or have not completed what they have been asked to do.

Scatterbrained. Lacks the power of concentration, or attention, flighty.

39 **Revengeful.** Knowingly or otherwise holds a grudge and punishes the offender, often by subtly withholding friendship or affection.

Restless. Likes constant new activity because it

isn't fun to do the same things all the time.

Reluctant. Unwilling or struggles against getting involved.

Rash. May act hastily, without thinking things through, generally because of impatience.

40 **Compromising.** Will often relax her position, even when right, in order to avoid conflict.

Critical. Constantly evaluating and making judgments, frequently thinking or expressing negative reactions.

Crafty. Shrewd, one who can always find a way to get to the desired end.

Changeable. A child-like, short attention span that needs a lot of change and variety to keep from getting bored.

Personality Scoring Sheet

Now transfer all your X's to the corresponding words on the Personality Scoring Sheet, and add up your totals. For example, if you checked Animated on the profile, check it on the scoring sheet. (Note: The words are in a different order on the profile and the scoring sheet.)

Strengths

	Popular Sanguine	Powerful Choleric	Perfect Melancholy	Peaceful Phlegmatic
1	Animated	Adventurous	Analytical	Adaptable
2	Playful	Persuasive	Persistent	Peaceful
3	Sociable	Strong-willed	Self-sacrificing	Submissive
4	Convincing	Competitive	Considerate	Controlled
5	Refreshing	Resourceful	Respectful	Reserved
6	Spirited	Self-reliant	Sensitive	Satisfied
7	Promoter	Positive	Planner	Patient
8	Spontaneous	Sure	Scheduled	Shy
9	Optimistic	Outspoken	Orderly	Obliging

In His Presents

10 Funny	Forceful	Faithful	Friendly
11 Delightful	Daring	Detailed	Diplomatic
12 Cheerful	Confident	Cultured	Consistent
13 Inspiring	Independent	Idealistic	Inoffensive
14 Demonstrative	Decisive	Deep	Dry humor
15 Mixes easily	Mover	Musical	Mediator
16 Talker	Tenacious	Thoughtful	Tolerant
17 Lively	Leader	Loyal	Listener
18 Cute	Chief	Chartmaker	Contented
19 Popular	Productive	Perfectionist	Pleasant
20 Bouncy	Bold	Behaved	Balanced

——————— ——————— ——————— ———————

(Totals — Strengths)

Weaknesses

Popular	Powerful	Perfect	Peaceful
Sanguine	Choleric	Melancholy	Phlegmatic

21 Brassy	Bossy	Bashful	Blank
22 Undisciplined	Unsympathetic	Unforgiving	Unenthusiastic
23 Repetitious	Resistant	Resentful	Reticent
24 Forgetful	Frank	Fussy	Fearful
25 Interrupts	Impatient	Insecure	Indecisive
26 Unpredictable	Unaffectionate	Unpopular	Uninvolved
27 Haphazard	Headstrong	Hard to please	Hesitant
28 Permissive	Proud	Pessimistic	Plain
29 Angered easily	Argumentative	Alienated	Aimless
30 Naive	Nervy	Negative attitude	Nonchalant
31 Wants credit	Workaholic	Withdrawn	Worrier
32 Talkative	Tactless	Too sensitive	Timid
33 Disorganized	Domineering	Depressed	Doubtful
34 Inconsistent	Intolerant	Introvert	Indifferent
35 Messy	Manipulative	Moody	Mumbles
36 Show-off	Stubborn	Skeptical	Slow
37 Loud	Lord over others	Loner	Lazy
38 Scatterbrained	Short-tempered	Suspicious	Sluggish

39 Restless	Rash	Revengeful	Reluctant
40 Changeable	Crafty	Critical	Compromising

_____	_____	_____	_____

(Totals — Weaknesses)

_____	_____	_____	_____

(Totals — Strengths)

_____	_____	_____	_____

Combined Totals

"The Personality Profile," created by Fred Littauer, is from *After Every Wedding Comes a Marriage* by Florence Littauer. Copyright © 1981, Harvest House Publishers. Used by permission.

Once you've transferred your answers to the scoring sheet, added up your total number of answers in each of the four columns, and added your totals from both the strengths and weaknesses sections, you'll know your dominant personality type. You'll also know what combination you are. If, for example, your score is 35 in Powerful Choleric strengths and weaknesses, there's really little question. You're almost all Powerful Choleric. But if your score is, for example, 16 in Powerful Choleric, 14 in Perfect Melancholy, and 5 in each of the others, you're a Powerful Choleric with a strong Perfect Melancholy. You'll also, of course, know your least dominant type.

To help you understand more about your Personality type, the following pages offer an overview of each Personality type.

Popular Sanguines
"Let's do it the fun way"
Desire: have fun

Emotional needs: attention, affection, approval, acceptance

Key strengths: ability to talk about anything at any time at any place, bubbling personality, optimism, sense of humor, storytelling ability, enjoyment of people

Key weaknesses: disorganized, can't remember details or names, exaggerates, not serious about anything, trusts others to do the work, too gullible and naive

Get depressed when: life is no fun and no one seems to love them

Are afraid of: being unpopular or bored, having to live by the clock, having to keep a record of money spent

Like people who: listen and laugh, praise and approve

Dislike people who: criticize, don't respond to their humor, don't think they are cute

Are valuable in work for: colorful creativity, optimism, light touch, cheering up others, entertaining

Could improve if they: got organized, didn't talk so much, learned to tell time

As leaders they: excite, persuade, and inspire others; exude charm and entertain; are forgetful and poor on follow-through

Tend to marry: Perfect Melancholies who are sensitive and serious, but whom they quickly tire of having to cheer up and by whom they soon tire of being made to feel inadequate or stupid

Reaction to stress: leave the scene, go shopping, find a fun group, create excuses, blame others

Recognized by their: constant talking, loud volume, bright eyes

Powerful Cholerics
"Let's do it my way"

Desire: have control

Emotional needs: sense of obedience, appreciation for accomplishments, credit for ability

Key strengths: ability to take charge of anything instantly and to make quick, correct judgments

Key weaknesses: too bossy, domineering, autocratic, insensitive, impatient, unwilling to delegate or give credit to others

Get depressed when: life is out of control and people won't do things their way

Are afraid of: losing control of anything (e.g., losing a job, not being promoted, becoming seriously ill, having a rebellious child or unsupportive mate)

Like people who: are supportive and submissive, see things their way, cooperate quickly, let them take credit

Dislike people who: are lazy and not interested in working constantly, buck their authority, become independent, aren't loyal

Are valuable in work because they: can accomplish more than anyone else in a shorter time, are usually right

Could improve if they: allowed others to make decisions, delegated authority, became more patient, didn't expect everyone to produce as they do

As leaders they have: a natural feel for being in charge, a quick sense of what will work, a sincere belief in their ability to achieve, a potential to overwhelm less aggressive people

Tend to marry: Peaceful Phlegmatics who will quietly obey and not buck their authority, but who never accomplish enough or get excited over their projects

Reaction to stress: tighten control, work harder, exercise more, get rid of the offender

Recognized by their: fast-moving approach, quick grab for control, self-confidence, restless and overpowering attitude

Perfect Melancholies
"Let's do it the right way"
Desire: have it right
Emotional needs: sense of stability, space, silence,

sensitivity, support
Key strengths: ability to organize and set long-range goals, have high standards and ideals, analyze deeply
Key weaknesses: easily depressed, too much time on preparation, too focused on details, remembers negatives, suspicious of others
Get depressed when: life is out of order, standards aren't met, and no one seems to care
Are afraid of: no one understanding how they really feel, making a mistake, having to compromise standards
Like people who: are serious, intellectual, deep, and will carry on a sensible conversation
Dislike people who: are lightweights, forgetful, late, disorganized, superficial, prevaricating, and unpredictable
Are valuable in work for: sense of detail, love of analysis, follow-through, high standards of performance, compassion for the hurting
Could improve if they: didn't take life quite so seriously, didn't insist others be perfectionists
As leaders they: organize well, are sensitive to people's feelings, have deep creativity, want quality performance
Tend to marry: Popular Sanguines for their outgoing personality and social skills, but whom they soon attempt to quiet and get on a schedule
Reaction to stress: withdraw, get lost in a book, become depressed, give up, recount the problems
Recognized by their: serious and sensitive nature, well-mannered approach, self-deprecating comments, meticulous and well-groomed looks

Peaceful Phlegmatic
"Let's do it the easy way"
Desire: avoid conflict, keep peace
Emotional needs: sense of respect, feeling of worth, understanding, emotional support

Key strengths: balance, even disposition, dry sense of humor, pleasing personality

Key weaknesses: lack of decisiveness, enthusiasm, and energy; a hidden will of iron

Get depressed when: life is full of conflict, they have to face a personal confrontation, no one wants to help, the buck stops with them

Are afraid of: having to deal with a major personal problem, being left holding the bag, making major changes

Like people who: will make decisions for them, will recognize their strengths, will not ignore them, will give them respect

Dislike people who: are too pushy, too loud, and expect too much of them

Are valuable in work because they: mediate between contentious people, objectively solve problems

Could improve if they: set goals and became self-motivated, were willing to do more and move faster than expected, could face their own problems as well as they handle those of others

As leaders they: keep calm, cool, and collected; don't make impulsive decisions; are well-liked and inoffensive; won't cause trouble; don't often come up with brilliant new ideas

Tend to marry: Powerful Cholerics who are strong and decisive, but by whom they soon tire of being pushed around and looked down upon

Reaction to stress: hide from it, watch TV, eat, tune out life

Recognized by their: calm approach, relaxed posture (sitting or leaning when possible)

In His Presents

6

That's Nice, Now What Do I Do With It?

You've all experienced it. You open the gift, say thank you, and then go home and think *I will never use that.* That happened to me with one of our wedding gifts. It was a warming tray from one of our grooms-men, George Cizek. I had never seen one, and, there-fore, didn't think I would ever use it. So, I packed it back in the box and put it in our storage room.

Tommy and I honeymooned from Saturday until the following Wednesday. He had to get back and help with the farming, and so I set about to begin my wifely chore of cooking. Mama usually had dinner ready by about 5:30 or 6:00, so I thought that's what I should do too. At 5:30, the food was ready, but Tommy wasn't home. At 6:00, he still wasn't home. When it turned 7:00 and there was still no sign of Tommy, I thought that warm-ing tray might come in pretty handy. It was only after that night that Tommy explained to his city girl that farmers don't come in for supper at 5:30.

What I thought would be an unused gift became in-valuable. What I thought I'd never need, instead be-came essential on a daily basis. The handle is broken, one of the legs is missing, but twenty-seven years later I'm still using the same tray.

That's what I want to happen with your knowledge of the personalities. I want you to take it out, use it, see the benefits of it, and put it to work for the honor and glory of God. Review chapter three if you need a reminder about the reasons for studying the personalities in the first place.

Communicating With Personality

"If it be possible, as much as lieth in you, live peaceably with all men" (Romans 12:18). We are instructed to do what we can to get along with others. To me, that means not only trying to understand others' points of view, but also trying to meet their needs according to what is essential for their peace of mind. Let's look at some pointers shared by Linda Jewell of CLASServices on how to communicate more effectively out of our personality style and taking the temperaments of others into consideration.

We observed that the basic *desire* of Sanguines is to have fun. While this is their desire, the *need* behind it is one for attention and approval. They are very people-oriented and require our interest. That means when you are with Sanguines, you should try your best not to tune them out. Tell these people stories with colorful details to best engage them in what you are trying to get across.

If you are a Sanguine, truly concentrate on toning down. Limit your wordiness and realize that other people have something to say too. Practice listening, especially to other people's names, as you are being introduced. And one last thing, if you are interrupted while telling one of your famous stories, only continue if asked.

What about Cholerics? We've established that they *desire* control, but they *need* appreciation. Even though they are project oriented, they still thrive when others say, "You really did a good job. I don't know how you do all that you do."

If you are wanting to communicate with a Powerful Personality, remember Jack Webb's motto on the television series *Drag Net*. "Just the facts, Ma'am. Just the facts." They don't want all of the cute stories and gory details. Save those for the Populars. They are not into chitchat. Keep it to the point and give them the bottom line first.

As a Choleric, you must concentrate on your tone of voice. It often sounds like you're mad at the world. There have been many times when I have wounded the spirit of my sweet, Phlegmatic Jill, not by what I said but by the way I said it. You need to learn to request, not demand. Don't finish others' sentences and try your best to focus on the person, not the project she is doing for you.

When conversing with Melancholies, keep in mind that their basic *desire* is perfection, but their basic *need* is sensitivity. It is the *way* things are done that is most important to them. They function on a need-to-know basis, so when approaching them for conversation, respect their time, space, and schedule. Ask if it's a good time to talk and if so, fill them with details. Don't try to jolly them up, but do laugh or cry with them.

If you are a Melancholy, you must adjust your expectations. No one is perfect and others get extremely frustrated trying to live up to but never quite meeting your standards. Celebrate small improvements and give praise instead of constant criticism. It will take practice, but make positive observations instead of always finding fault.

Finally, the Peaceful Phlegmatics are pacification oriented and have a basic *desire* for peace, but their basic *need* is to have feelings of worth. When you are trying to connect with them, give them your undivided attention. Verbalize your appreciation for them. In conversation, wait to speak until they're completely finished. If it comes to giving them choices on something, give only a few. It frustrates them to make a decision!

As a Phlegmatic, learn to express your opinion. Rehearse speaking up and showing enthusiasm with your body language. Practice making choices because it irritates others when you don't.[1]

Let's Get Personal

Okay, we've learned to "do unto others as they would have us do unto them." By zeroing in on communication, we've tried to see how we can speak the language the listener understands so that we may *"live peaceably with all men"* (Romans 12:18).

As difficult as that may seem and as hard as that is to put into practice, our most complex endeavor is dealing with another personality — our own. Psalm 139 revealed that each of us must allow God to expose the things in our lives that need changing and then allow Him to change them. The *Life Application Study Bible* commentary says that David is actually asking God to do exploratory surgery for sin.[2]

Have you ever had exploratory surgery? I have, and it is pretty invasive. They cut you open and look around to see what might be causing the problem. We don't want them to find out what is wrong just for informational purposes, and then sew us back up without correcting it. The whole purpose is to expose the problem so it can be corrected.

That is what David was asking God to do. That is what Jesus said we must do.

Psalm 139
"Search me and know my *heart.*"

Matthew 22:37
"Love the Lord with all thy *heart.*"

"Try me and know my *thoughts*."	"Love the Lord with all thy *mind*."
"See if there be any wicked *way* in me."	"Love the Lord with all thy *soul*."

Every part of our being must be willingly exposed to God so He can do the work of conforming us to the image of His Son. That is His ultimate will for us all.

When the Bible speaks about the *way* of a man, I believe it is talking about the very essence of who we are — our soul, our will, our chooser. The part of me that makes me me. Psalm 37:5 instructs us to *"Commit thy way unto the LORD."* Proverbs 22:6 tells us to *"train up a child in the way he should go."* This *way* is our individuality, our personality, our uniqueness.

As you went through the personality profile, did God reveal to you any character weaknesses? What did you do with that revelation? If this is exploratory surgery, you need to repent of those, focus on Him, and let Him remove them. Each time He reveals another personality flaw, repent and focus on Him. This revelation/repentance cycle is one way God uses to draw you into a closer relationship to Him.

Too often we think it is our weaknesses that hinder us most in our relationship with the Father. But let this Choleric make a confession to you all just now. My strengths cause me the most problems. Why? I know my shortcomings and go immediately to the Father for help with those. But my strengths: *Why goodness, Lord, You know I can handle those things myself! No need to bother You. I'm really good at this and won't be needing Your help any today.* It is what I feel the most confident in that should bring me to my knees, because that is nothing but pride, which is listed first in Solomon's Top Seven List of Things God Hates the Most! (Proverbs 6:16-19).

Just My Size

One of the downsides to our family's Christmas celebration is the day after. For us, that meant taking down all of the decorations and, all too often, going back to the mall and exchanging the things that didn't fit. That's not the case with our personalities. Believe it or not, they are just our size. We may have too much confidence in our strengths or be too upset over our weaknesses, but remember God made us just the way we are.

Why? He knew exactly what it would take to draw each of us into a closer relationship with Him. The traits He uses in your life may be totally opposite to what He uses in mine, but all of them are to make us more like Jesus.

Our personality affects every part of our lives, even the way we approach our relationship with Him. Each of us must come to God through repentance and a saving knowledge of Jesus Christ, but I don't imagine there are any two of us who have identical conversion experiences. Some may have cried; some may have laughed; some may have shown no emotion. Some may have come the first time they heard the gospel, and others only after years of putting Him off. This, too, is part of our personality.

Remember when we looked at our position as a child of God? Compare this experience to establishing a relationship with your own children. Suppose, as a parent, you wanted a daily, ongoing, thriving relationship with each of your offspring. To establish this relationship you approach them this way. "I expect to talk to each of you today. If you wish to talk to me you must get up very early and do so before you do anything else. Plan to spend at least fifteen to thirty minutes with me during which time we will discuss everything about your day — school, work, friends, financial matters, health issues, problems — everything. We will repeat this process again every day, same time, same place, same way. Oh, and if you want to check in with me for a few minutes before you go to bed, that will be permissible."

Isn't that crazy? Yet isn't that exactly what we think God expects us to do in our relationship with Him? We think we must have a quiet time at a certain part of the day, for a certain length of time, and we must read *X* amount of scriptures. If we don't, we somehow feel we have miserably failed in trying to connect with Him.

Ladies, nowhere does the Bible say we have to read it through in one year. Nowhere does the Bible say we have to have a certain posture when we pray. Nowhere does the Bible set one time frame or method for being in His presence, and we certainly aren't required to address Him only in King James English!

Our means of worshiping God are as varied as our personalities. There is probably not a Sanguine that can spend fifteen minutes straight talking to God. Yet there are many Sanguines that don't go fifteen minutes *without* talking to God. They have an ongoing conversation with Him throughout their day and probably do better than the rest of us to *"pray without ceasing"* (1 Thessalonians 5:17).

The Cholerics will likely use devotional books to direct their thoughts for the day. As they confront their to-do list, they probably send up *flash* prayers for strength to face the next project. Being goal-oriented, they may view their quiet time as another objective to be pursued.

The Melancholies are the ones most apt to set aside an extended time communing with God. They will often journal and may even have notebooks full of prayers they have penned. On the other hand, the Phlegmatics are usually the ones who will quietly dwell in His presence throughout the day.

Ladies, don't be guilty of thinking your way to worship is *the* way to worship. Don't look down your nose at those who don't rise at dawn or kneel to pray. And don't feel guilty if this is not your way of having a quiet time. Our guilt should not come in how we individually worship and build our relationship to God, but only if we are not in any way trying to establish this relationship. Your quiet time should be perfectly suited to you. It should be just your size.

Unwrapping the Gift

Below are some scriptures that may be helpful for each personality type. Read the ones in your category, meditate on them, and write what the Lord has taught you through these verses.

Sanguine
Proverbs 11:13; 13:3; 15:2; 20:19; 29:11, 20; Ecclesiastes 5:2; 9:17; James 1:19

_____

_____

_____

Choleric
Proverbs 15:1; 16:3; 29:11, 22-23; Galatians 5:22-26; James 1:19; 1 John 1:9

_____

_____

_____

Melancholy
Proverbs 17:22; Romans 12:3; 14:4; Philippians 2:3;

4:6-8; Colossians 3:12-15; James 4:12

_____

_____

_____

Phlegmatic
Proverbs 29:25; Ecclesiastes 9:10; Colossians 3:23-24;
2 Timothy 1:7; 2 Peter 1:5-8

_____

_____

_____

1. Information from this section was adapted from a handout developed by Linda Jewell for CLASServices Inc.

2. *Life Application Study Bible.* Wheaton, Illinois: Tyndale House Publishers, Inc. 1067.

In His Presents

The Present of Our Participation in His Church

$Okay$, ladies, it's review time. Let's look back over all of the *spiffy* gifts the Lord has given us so far.

He has *saved* us to give us our *position* in Christ.

He has *selected* each part of our *personality* and talents to uniquely qualify us.

Now let's see how He has a *service* for each of us to *participate* in as part of His church.

God wants us to be the best we can be. He knew that to do so would mean being part of His church. He wants to:

B Build His Church
E Evangelize the World
S Strengthen His People
T Transform Lives

Our gift is that He wants us to have a part in all of that.

Participation includes three major aspects — to take part in, to share, or to be related to a larger whole.[1] All of these aspects are applicable when you think about involvement in the church. When we take part in, we're active in the support of the services and ministries of the church. To share has a more personal connotation. Instead of an active level, participation reaches us on an emotional level where we are called to "bear one another's burdens." Then to relate to a larger whole helps us to see how we are all connected to all other parts of our church family.

Psalm 68:6 tells us, *"God setteth the solitary in families."* He doesn't leave us alone to fend for ourselves. He means for us to be part of a local body of believers where we can bond with one another and become all that He means for us to be. Participation in His church provides fellowship and interaction with other believers, training, and opportunities for service.

God doesn't lead us to a church only for what we can glean; He leads us to one in which we can give our time, our talents, our tithes, and ourselves. Have you ever said, "That church just doesn't have anything for me and my family"? Have you ever thought that maybe God is leading you there for what you have to offer them? If God is truly directing you to join a certain church, you had better believe He has a place for you to fill, and it's not just the pew! It's a match similar to the one you experience in a marriage. Usually your mate has strong points in areas where you are the weakest and vice versa. Together you combine and fill each others' voids so that you can be a complete whole.

God wants you to help complete your local church. You have strengths, weaknesses, needs, desires, things you can do, and things you can't. How awesome that He would place you in a church body so you can fill in some low places and at the same time get your cup filled as well. Oh, He may ask you to do things you don't feel very confident in undertaking. He may ask you to work outside of your comfort zone, but remember this, our comfort is not His first priority, our obedience is.

Florence Littauer says, "God usually gifts us along the line of our personality patterns unless He calls us to a ministry for which we are not fit. Then He gifts us to fit the call."[2] That takes away any excuse! We can't say, "I'm not good at this," or "I'm not equipped to handle that," or "I just can't."

Well, no, we're not, and no, we can't, but God is, and God can. He is the One Who made us. He is the One Who equips us. He is the One Who gifts us. He is the One Who calls us. And since we know we cannot do this ourselves, then God gets the glory.

"For ye see your calling, brethren, how that not many wise men after the flesh, not many mighty, not many noble, are called: but God hath chosen the foolish things of the world to confound the wise; and God hath chosen the weak things of the world to confound the things which are mighty; and base things of the world, and things which are despised, hath God chosen, yea, and things which are not, to bring to nought things that are: that no flesh should glory in his presence. But of him are ye in Christ Jesus, who of God is made unto us wisdom, and righteousness, and sanctification, and redemption: that, according as it is written, He that glorieth, let him glory in the Lord" (1 Corinthians 1:26-31).

Don't you know God has heard them all, excuses that is. We ought to just number them or call them by their scripture reference or the Bible character who used them first. What we are actually doing is just recycling old excuses.

Jeremiah said he couldn't speak. God said, *"I have put my words in thy mouth"* (Jeremiah 1:9).

Moses used the same excuse and told the Lord he wasn't a speaker. This time God gave His servant someone to do that for him, his brother Aaron.

Gideon said, "I am poor, the least of my father's house." God simply said, *"I will be with thee"* (Judges 6:15-16).

Amos was worried about what others would think. After all, he was just a herdsman. Who would listen to him? Moses used that excuse too. He protested that the people would not believe him and would question who sent him. God said, "Tell them I AM hath sent you." Let's see if they will argue with that!

But melancholy, worrisome Moses still had his doubts and his excuses complaining that he didn't have the means necessary to do what God wanted him to do. God asked, "What is in thine hand?" And it was a rod. It was nothing unusual or out of the ordinary, but simply a tool of Moses' trade. It was something he had used on a daily basis for forty years. But now God wanted it. God wanted Moses to relinquish it to Him. And when Moses gave God his ordinary shepherd's rod, He turned it into an extraordinary tool of power and deliverance.

A Look Back

For some examples of how God can use people and their gifts in His service, let's look at some not-too-familiar Old Testament characters.

In Exodus 25:8, God said, *"Let them make me a sanctuary; that I may dwell among them."* In other words, God wanted an actual, physical structure where He could meet with His people, accept their sacrifices and offerings, and dwell among them. The antecedent of *them* in this scripture is the children of Israel. God had something for all of them to do, but He also got very specific.

That's where Bezaleel, Aholiab, and Ithamar come in. What? You don't know Bezaleel, Aholiab, and Ithamar? Didn't you want to name your children after these men?

No? Well good! That is my point exactly.

It doesn't matter if you are well known or recognized and remembered for what you do. God wants us to fulfill our part of His work during our time in history. It is not the recognition or results we should be concerned about, but our response to God's call and direction.

Let's examine Exodus 31 to see some of the main participants in the tabernacle building project. We will see Moses, Bezaleel, Aholiab, Ithamar, some unnamed people, and then the children of Israel in general. God called all of them, gave each a specific task, and made all of them important to the cause.

We start in verse one with Moses. The Lord was speaking to Moses directly. What He was sharing with him was part of the forty-day conversation they had. (That's why I say Moses had to be a Melancholy to remember all of those details.) Moses was the recipient of God's message, and he was expected to share it with others. Notice two important points here. You may be the one to whom God speaks and He expects you to relay the message, or God may be sending you a message through another person and He expects you to listen.

In verse two, we meet Bezaleel. God was very specific. He called him by name, and just in case the name Bezaleel was the boy name of the year in Israel at that time, he pinpointed the exact Bezaleel He was talking about — the son of Uri, the son of Hur, of the tribe of Judah. Oh, that Bezaleel. There was no question who God was talking about. God knew, Moses knew, and Bezaleel knew. Do you ever question God's call and direction in your life? I think we usually know it's Him, but we try to ignore it. He is very specific. It is Satan who speaks in generalities. It is God Who lets us know exactly what He has in mind.

Not only did God call him by name, but He filled him with His Spirit. When God calls, He equips. With Moses, it was a spokesperson and a rod. Just look at this impressive list of God's qualifications for Bezaleel. God filled him with the Spirit of God *"in wisdom, and in understanding, and in knowledge, and in all manner of workmanship"* (Exodus 31:3). The wisdom, understanding, and knowledge all seem a little abstract. But look at that last one. He was filled with God's Spirit in work-manship. To be even more specific verses 4 and 5 tell us, *"To devise cunning works, to work in gold, and in silver, and in brass, and in cutting of stones, to set them, and in carving of timber, to work in all manner of work-manship."*

So, let me get this straight. Bezaleel wasn't just a Spirit-filled man who simply existed in the nation of Is-rael to bless them with his presence, but he was a con-tractor, so to speak, whose work and the craft of his hands showed the power of God in his life. Yes, *yes,* and again I say YES! God used his talents, his abilities, his skill, and his craft to bring honor and glory in the building of the tabernacle. He also used him to teach others to do the same (Exodus 35:34).

Oh ladies, what an example Bezaleel gives us. Is it washing clothes and cooking meals? Is it teaching school or keeping books? Is it keeping the nursery or leading GMAs? Whatever it is, if God has called us to that position, He will fill us with His Spirit and the abil-ity to do it so that He can get the honor and glory.

Next, in Exodus 31, we meet Aholiab. The first thing we notice about him is that God gave him to Bezaleel. Just glance through the chapters leading up to this one and read all of the details of the tabernacle and the fur-nishings that were to go inside. If you were Bezaleel and Moses was telling you all that needed to be done, what would your first reaction be? *I need help!* But before he could even ask, God provided. It is not until chapter 38 in verses 22 and 23 that we find out more about Aholiab. He was an engraver, an embroiderer of cloth.

Now I don't know for sure, ladies, but it sounds to me like Bezaleel did the major design and construction, and then the detail work was left for Aholiab. Isn't that neat. Some of us are big picture people and organizers, while others would rather do the detail work of making the big picture come together. God is so good to pair us with each other so that together we can make sure it is all completed.

Then we meet the unnamed. In verse 6 God said, *"and in the hearts of all that are wise hearted I have put wisdom, that they may make all that I have commanded thee."* These workers were only known as wise hearted, but that was enough. They received the privilege of helping build the tabernacle, the ark, the mercy seat, all of the furniture, the candlestick, the altar, the lavers, the garments for Aaron and his sons, and even the anointing oil and incense that was to be used in the holy place.

Now there is something I don't want you to miss. Who were the instructions given to? Moses. Twice God said these people were to make all that God had commanded *Moses* to do. Now what do you make of that? Would we be inclined to say, "Hey, Moses. God told you to do this, not me," or in other words, "That's not my job"? Not these people. Remember, they were wise hearted, and Jeremiah 9:23-24 states that a truly wise man will glory in his understanding and knowledge of God. They didn't care who got the credit as long as God got the glory. Moses was their leader, the one God had put over them. The job was his, but he had the authority to enlist help to get it done. God equipped the people to do just that. Part of their job was to follow their leader. They did so willingly and with wise hearts.

Next, we meet Ithamar. Exodus 38:21-23 and Numbers 4:21-28 show us that he was in charge of overseeing the assembly and disassembly of the tabernacle as the nation moved from place to place. God was the architect; Moses was the foreman; Ithamar was the construction manager; Bezaleel was the head carpenter; Aholiab was the finish man.

But we're not through. To do all of this, they needed materials, supplies, and finances. Exodus 35:29 and

36:6-7 tells us that, *"The children of Israel brought a willing offering unto the LORD, every man and woman, whose heart made them willing to bring for all manner of work."* In fact, so much was brought that they had to restrain them because they had brought too much. Can you imagine not having to take up an offering in church because everyone had already given too much? Wow! That boggles my mind.

Those who were good at overseeing, oversaw. Those who were good at delegating, delegated. Those who could do carpentry, built. Those who could engrave or sew, engraved and sewed. Others brought all the materials that were needed for each job. Each had a role. Each had a place. Each had a job. And each of them did it so that God could have a sanctuary where He might dwell among them.

Now it is our turn, ladies. He has a job for us. He has a role for us to fill. He has a place of service for each of us, and it is all because He wants to dwell among us, to live within us, to empower each of us so that as His church we can build up, evangelize, strengthen each other, and transform lives for His honor and glory.

1. God had a specific task:
   - He called specific people.
   - He equipped them with specific talents and abilities.
   - He supported them with other people to help them.
   - He supplied them with materials brought by other people.
   - He instructed them as to what to do.
2. God used specific people.
   - Moses received the plans from God.
   - Bezaleel and Aholiab carried out the plans.
   - Ithamar supervised the setting up and tearing down of the tabernacle.
   - The wise hearted served as assistants.

- The children of Israel made the provisions so the plans could be carried out.

3. God gave specific results:
   - The people did as God commanded.
   - Moses blessed them (Exodus 39:42-43).
   - Moses finished the work (Exodus 40:1, 16, 33-34).
   - Then the glory of the Lord filled the temple.

That is the ultimate present of participation, to be filled with God's glory. We may never receive recognition, appreciation, or attention. After all, none of us were very familiar with these men and the work they did on the tabernacle. But they fulfilled their place in God's timetable during their moment in history. May it ever be our goal to do the same.

Unwrapping the Gift

1. Bezaleel and Aholiab were called by God. Read the following scripture and share about what it means for you to be *"called."*

Romans 8:28 _____

1 Corinthians 1:9 _____

1 Peter 2:9-10 _____

2. God filled these men with His Spirit so that they might accomplish the task He had given them to do. Study the following passages on filling.

Ephesians 3:14-21
   How do we receive strength to do what He has given us to do?

_____

What will that enable us to do? _____

How will God be glorified? _____

Summarize what this passage means about you, your relationship to God, and serving Him through the church.

_____

Ephesians 5:14-20

What specific things mentioned in this passage would make it obvious to those around us that we are *"filled"* with the Spirit?

_____

Philippians 1:9-11

What things did Paul pray for the Philippian church in this passage?

_____

What is the ultimate end of these attributes?

_____

Colossians 1:9-12

List the things Paul said would result from being *"filled with the knowledge of his will in all wisdom and spiritual understanding."*

_____

3. Do you feel you know what God has *called* you to do within His church? If so, what?

_____

1. Webster, page 614.

2. Florence Littauer. Personality Plus Training, P.O. Box 66810, Albuquerque NM 87120.

8

The Who's, What's, and Why's of the Spiritual Gifts

First Corinthians 3:16 says, *"Know ye not that ye are the temple of God, and that the Spirit of God dwelleth in you?"* Isn't that an awesome thought! We spent the entire last chapter seeing how God instructed the Israelites to build Him a tabernacle so that He could dwell among them. Now, fast forward to the New Testament, and we find God telling us we *are* the temple of God *because His Spirit already dwells in us.* Wow!

He took great pains in directing His people on every detail of the tabernacle's construction and furnishings. Shouldn't we assume that He wants to be the overseer of our individual temples as well? He cleansed it for us with the blood of His Son. He furnishes it with just what we need to worship Him, serve Him, and glorify Him. He is the ultimate interior designer. He keeps our individuality in mind as well as His desired decorating scheme for our lives when He equips us with exactly what we need to be conformed to the image of Jesus Christ. He is with us and empowers us to do whatever He calls us to do.

The tabernacle teaches us some great lessons for our

individual temples, and our churches. In Exodus, God had:

A Specific Purpose: "*Make me a sanctuary; that I may dwell among them*" (Exodus 25:8).

A Specific People: Aholiab and Bezaleel were called out by name to do their particular job (Exodus 31:2, 6).

A Specific Product: The people were blessed and God's glory filled the temple (Exodus 40:34).

The same is true in the Great Commission to the church found in Matthew 28:18-20. Jesus gave us direct instruction to accomplish His plan.

A Specific Purpose. "*Go ye therefore, and teach.*" We must evangelize the world and bring it to a saving knowledge of Jesus Christ. "*Baptizing them.*" We must strengthen them through obedience to Christ and identification with the Lord. "*Teaching them to observe.*" We are to train and build up the church by increasing new believers' understanding of God's Word and by helping to shape their will to conform to His.

This last *teaching* has always convicted me. He tells His disciples to teach *them,* the new believers, "*to observe all things whatsoever I have commanded you.*" Now, I don't know for sure, but I feel there is a reason He didn't say "teaching them to observe all things whatsoever I have commanded them." Do you see the difference? His emphasis is on His disciples. They were to obey. They were to live out the dedicated, separated life so that the new converts could learn and grow by watching those already in the church be obedient to the commands of God. The disciples weren't just to give the new believers a list of rules and tell them to follow them. They were to *demonstrate* them. As Oswald Chambers said, "We can't make disciples unless we are disciples ourselves."[1]

A Specific People. If we are a part of His church, then we are part of "an assembly of people called out from the world by the preaching of the gospel accompanied by the regenerative work of the Holy Spirit and baptized in faith and fellowship of the gospel, to a life of conformation to the will of God and to execute the will and perpetuate the ordinance of Christ until He comes."[2]

That is heavy duty! The Lord's church is not just called out *from* the world, but called *to* conform to and carry out God's will.

A Specific Product. Building the tabernacle brought God's blessing and presence to the people. The Great Commission brings the same blessing to the church. *"Lo, I am with you alway."* There could be no greater blessing than to know that we have the constant, uninterrupted presence of God in our lives. His presence is the ultimate glory that can be experienced this side of heaven.

We know the result of our relationship to God. We know we are His people. We know He has a purpose for each of us as individuals. Let's examine just how He equips each of us to fulfill that purpose.

In His Presents

Think how you would feel in this experience.

You have a friend who lives in a city many, many miles away; and because of this great distance, you haven't been able to see each other for years. Every Christmas, though, you try to make up for that distance by taking great care and effort in choosing just the right gift. Even the details of the wrapping reflect your love and respect for your friend, as you select elegant paper and colorful, exquisite bows.

Then one day, out of the blue, someone sends you enough money to make a long-dreamed-of visit to your friend. Bubbling with anticipation, you travel the many miles, finally reveling in your friend's warm welcome. Talking and laughing like two giddy kids, you share a wonderful ride from the airport, until at last you've arrived at your friend's home. After a few moments, you pause to survey the living room, but see none of your gifts on display. While still chatting, you glance into the den, the kitchen, the hallway — no gifts. Your heart begins to sink, but you don't have the courage to ask about the gifts.

While your friend is away on an errand, however, you peek into the front closet, and your heart drops. There, after all these years, are all the once-glittering gifts you sent, still wrapped and unused. How would you feel?[3]

How would you feel? Hurt? Frustrated? Angry? Confused? Sad? It would be the same as if we had bought Christmas presents every year for our own children and they never bothered to open them. Yet day after day, week after week, Sunday after Sunday, and year after year God's children sit in the pews of His churches unfulfilled and unmotivated because they haven't bothered to open up their spiritual gifts and find out exactly what is in His presents to them.

There is so much confusion about the gifts. There are so many doubts, and there is so much false humility. We spend our time saying, "I don't think I have any gifts." Or, "Mrs. So-N-So can do so much, but I can't think of anything I can do." As my Granny Cobb would say, "Hogwash!"

God gives us not one, but four different passages in His Word to help us understand and clarify the practice of the spiritual gifts. We have, therefore, no excuse for not finding our place of service and then fulfilling it.

Before we look at what the spiritual gifts are, let's make sure we understand what they are *not*. The gifts of the Spirit are not the same as the *gift* of the Spirit. The third person of the Trinity comes to indwell us at the moment of salvation. We may not always be filled with the Spirit, but we are always indwelt by the Spirit.

The gifts of the Spirit are not the same as the *fruit* of the Spirit. The fruit of the Spirit is an expression of our spiritual condition and our relationship to God that shows itself in our attitude toward others. It is our character and response to the world around us. Dr. Michael Youssef says, "Fruit defines what a Christian is; gifts define what a Christian does."[4]

The gifts of the Spirit are not the same as a *talent*. A talent is a natural potential we are born with that usually has to be developed and trained. For example, some people who play the piano are simply striking notes while others are making music. You know of people who have a natural propensity for music and when they sing or play an instrument, they can lead you into worship. They have a natural, musical talent.

Other examples could be a natural talent for art and creativity. I can't draw a stick figure using a ruler. Others I know can create the most beautiful scenes with a pencil or pen. We have two ladies in our church who are wonderful at decorating for all of our special events. Edna and Tammie can take a box, drape it with net or gold lamé, scatter leaves around it and voilà, a beautiful centerpiece! That is a natural talent. I try it and it looks like a box with net or gold lamé and leaves scattered around.

What about physical talent? I don't know, but I'm pretty sure that I could probably practice basketball twelve hours a day, six days a week and still not be able to dunk it like Michael Jordan. He has a natural talent.

Natural talent is present in the saved and unsaved alike. It has nothing to do with our spiritual life except those of us who are His children need to acknowledge that He enables us to have and develop those as well. We must recognize that all we have comes from Him and should be given back to Him.

What They Are

If we now know what they are not, let's look at some definitions of what the spiritual gifts are.

"Supernatural endowment, divinely-conferred ability by which the Holy Spirit enables a believer to serve God effectively in spiritual ministry" (E. Harold Henderson).[5]

"Skill or ability that enables each Christian to perform a function in the body of Christ with ease and effectiveness for the glory of God" (Charles Swindoll).[6]

"Energizing drive within us through which we are to carry out the ministry God has given us to do" (Charles Stanley).[7]

"Specific, Spirit-given ability that enables us to contribute to the wider good of the church, which in turn reaches out to the community and eventually the world" (*Serendipity*).[8]

A special aptitude and motivation given to each believer by God the Father, Son, and Holy Spirit at the moment of salvation that enables us to encourage, equip, and edify fellow believers as well as evangelize and enlighten the world at large. That's my definition. But it is not so much what we have to say about the spiritual gifts that matters, it's what God says. He is, after all, the expert on the subject.

As we read through the four major Bible passages that speak about the spiritual gifts I want you to see Who gave the gift, to whom it was given, why it was given, what the gift was, and other important points about the passage. (You may use the chart provided at the end of this chapter to organize this information.)

Romans 12. The *Life Application Bible* divides the book of Romans into two major divisions. Chapters 1-11 describe what to believe, and chapters 12-16 describe how to behave.[9] Beginning in Chapter 12, Paul shares the personal responsibility each of us has in living the life God intended. In the first section of this important chapter, he urges us to present our bodies as living sacrifices unto the Lord and then he immediately follows that with the passage on spiritual gifts. This is no coincidence. God inspired this book word-by-word. He means for us to see that our use of the gifts He has given us is one way of being totally submissive to Christ. Let's examine this passage for the answers to the questions we posed earlier.

By Whom: *"God hath dealt"* (verse 3).

To Whom: *"to every man"* (verse 3).

Why: So that a believer should not *"think of himself more highly than he ought to think;... For as we have many members in one body, and all members have not the same office: so we, being many, are one body in Christ"* (verses 3-5).

What: *"the measure of faith"* (verse 3); prophecy (verse 6); exhortation (verse 8); mercy (verse 8); ministry (verse 7); giving (verse 8); teaching (verse 7); ruling (verse 8).

God has given the gifts. If we are jealous of what someone else can do and upset at what we cannot do, then we are rebelling against God. It was His decision. It was His prerogative on what to give to whom.

Everyone has at least one gift. No one can say, "I can't do anything" or "I don't think I have any gift." That is an affront to God. Notice throughout these passages how many times *every* and *each* is used. That means you!

The gifts differ so that we can work together to make a complete body. The idea is unity, not sameness.

1 Corinthians 12. The letter to the Corinthians from Paul was written to answer questions they had about a variety of topics. Along with his solution to their problems, Paul takes the opportunity to teach them about how they should conduct themselves in their worship services. He then addresses the topic of spiritual gifts. On this topic, he specifically says he does not want them to be ignorant. In other words, he doesn't want them "not to know" about this most important topic.[10]

By Whom: *"the same Spirit"* (verse 4); *"the same Lord"* (verse 5); *"the same God which worketh all in all"* (verse

6); *"one and the selfsame Spirit"* (verse 11).

To Whom: *"is given to every man"* (verse 7); *"dividing to every man severally as he will"* (verse 11).

Why: *"to profit withal"* (verse 7).

What: "the manifestation of the Spirit" (verse 7); word of wisdom, word of knowledge (verse 8); faith, healing (verse 9); miracles, prophecy, discerning of spirits, tongues, interpretation of tongues (verse 10); apostles, prophets, teachers, miracles, healings, helps, governments, tongues (verse 28); interpreting tongues (verse 30).

The spiritual gifts are diverse. There are differences in what each of us is given. These are determined by the Spirit, the Lord Jesus Christ, and God the Father. There is a reason we are all equipped as we are, and it all lies in the fact that it is simply what the Holy Trinity willed and designed for each of us in order that we may all profit (verses 4-7, 11).

First Corinthians 12 teaches that we cannot be all things or do all things. Therefore, whatever we do should be done totally out of the motivating power of love for God. That's why Paul immediately goes into his famous treatise on love in 1 Corinthians 13. It is in context connected to our use of our spiritual gifts.

Ephesians 4. In Romans, Paul addressed the spiritual gifts from the standpoint of our personal responsibility in service to God. In 1 Corinthians, he answered their questions about how the business and ministry of the church should be carried out. In Ephesians, we see the heart of the spiritual gifts. This letter to the church at Ephesus was one of love, and Paul was encouraging them in their unity to one another through their oneness in Christ. This passage gives us the most complete *why* as to the purpose of the gifts.

By Whom: *"the gift of Christ"* (verse 7).

To Whom: *"But unto every one of us is given grace"* (verse 7).

Why: *"Endeavoring to keep the unity of the Spirit in the bond of peace"* (verse 3); *"For the perfecting of the saints, for the work of the ministry, for the edifying of the body of Christ"* (verse 12).

What: *"grace"* (verse 7); *"apostles;... prophets;... evangelists;... pastors and teachers"* (verse 11).

The emphasis is unity. Spiritual gifts are never meant to be divisive or a source of jealousy or contention. Over and over, Paul talks about unity and gives us the basis on which the gifts are to be used: one body, one Spirit, one hope, one Lord, one faith, one baptism, one God. The three points in verse 12 give the most complete basis for the use of our spiritual gifts.

"For the perfecting of the saints." The word *"perfecting"* means "complete furnishing." Therefore using our own spiritual gifts helps to mature us as individuals and complete each other. We completely furnish our churches this way! It is similar to a marriage. We complete one another; we don't take the other's place. And we certainly don't want to be just alike or one of us wouldn't be necessary.

"For the work of the ministry." The purpose of the church is to go, teach, baptize, and teach again. This can best be done when each of us is doing our part in the church to carry out this commission in the most effective manner.

"For the edifying of the body of Christ." Our task is to build up, motivate, encourage, and enable each other to be the best we can be. We do this by using our own gifts and appreciating others as they use theirs.

Probably the best summary for this passage is found in verses 15 and 16. *"But speaking the truth in love, [we] may grow up into him in all things, which is the head, even Christ: from whom the whole body fitly joined together and compacted by that which every joint supplieth, according to the effectual working in the measure of every part, maketh increase of the body unto the edifying of itself in love."*

I'm a visual learner, so when I think about this verse I see a three dimensional puzzle. Every piece is designed for a particular spot, and it must go in that one spot in order for the other pieces to fit properly. When it is all in place, the parts are close and compact, each connecting to the other to make a completed, sturdy work. Even one missing piece causes a weakness in the entire structure. The finished product is a collection of individual pieces, but it is viewed as a whole. It is the *whole* that receives the praise and admiration.

That is how it should be in the church. We all have at least one gift. We all are placed in our churches specifically to use that gift so that we might grow up and mature in Christ, work in an effectual manner, and edify the whole church.

1 Peter 4. Our final passage on the spiritual gifts is penned by a different author, Peter. In this book he is addressing Jewish Christians who have been persecuted and are now scattered throughout Asia Minor. Wait a minute! I can understand Paul telling Christians about the spiritual gifts to encourage their service to Christ and their edification of the church, but these are people who are hurting and suffering. Why in the middle of all of this trouble would they receive a letter that has them think about the gift of ministry or the gift of teaching? Once again we see that the focus is on others. Let's examine how Peter states this truth.

By Whom: *"the manifold grace of God"* (verse 10); *"the ability which God giveth"* (verse 11).

To Whom: *"As every man hath received the gift"* (verse 10).

Why: *"minister the same one to another"* (verse 10); *"good stewards of the manifold grace of God"* (verse 10); *"that God in all things may be glorified"* (verse 11).

What: *"minister"* (verse 10); *"speak as the oracles of God"* (verse 11).

Only two gifts are listed in this passage, ministry and teaching. All of the gifts we have discussed can be categorized under these two main headings.

Another important point about the spiritual gifts is not so much that we can call ours by name, but that we are working for the Lord in our church fulfilling what He has given each of us to do.

If I am persecuted or suffering in any way, I think it is time for me to throw a pity party. Now, no one is invited to my party except me, but I certainly want others to at least know I'm having one. From 1 Peter we can see that if, during our trials and tribulations, we can focus on and help others, then our minds will be taken off of our own problems. Peter even tells us this will bring us joy (verse 13) and make us happy (verse 14). We cannot focus on others, help and serve them, and dwell on our own sufferings at the same time.

Once again we see that the gifts are not for notice and praise of what we can do, but for the glory of God (1 Peter 4:14, 16, 19).

Unwrapping the Gift

1. Oswald Chambers said, "We cannot make disciples unless we are disciples ourselves." What do you think is involved in being a disciple of Christ?

_____

2. Realizing the Great Commission was given to the church, look at its four sections and share in which area you feel best able to participate.

Go — live out the life of Christ.

Teach — bring others to a saving knowledge of Jesus.

Baptize — exhort to obedience to and identification with Christ.

Teach — increase their understanding of God's Word.

3. Using the five definitions of spiritual gifts given in this lesson as well as the other information we've studied, give your own summary of a spiritual gift.

_____

_____

4. After studying the four major passages on the gifts, what truth spoke to you most directly? Was it Who gave the gifts, to whom the gifts were given, why the gifts were given, or what gifts were given? Explain.

_____

_____

In the 1 Peter passage, only two divisions were given, speaking and ministering. Taking the list of gifts from the other three passages, categorize them under one of these two headings.

Speaking   **Ministering**

_____   _____

_____   _____

_____   _____

_____   _____

_____   _____

Which of these two do you feel is more your gift area? Why?

_____

Author's Note: In the remainder of our lessons, I will not be discussing the following gifts for the reasons given. *Apostles* — This gift was limited to New Testament times and had certain specifications (Acts 1:21-26). *Pastors* — I feel this is referring to the office of pastor, and is therefore only a man's gift (Titus 1:6). *Miracles, healing, tongues, interpretation of tongues* — I believe these sign gifts were used by God to authenticate ministries before the early New Testament believers had the completed Bible.

1. Chambers,Oswald. *My Utmost For His Highest.* Uhrichsville, Ohio: Barbour Publishing, Inc., 1963.

2. Cobb, J. E. *Cobb's Baptist Church Manual.* Little Rock, AR: Baptist Publishing House, 1979. 13.

3. Swindoll, Charles R. *He Gave Gifts.* Anaheim, CA: Insight for Living, 1992. 9.

4. Youssef, Michael. *Gifts of the Spirit.* Atlanta, GA: Leading the Way, 1998. 17.

5. Henderson, E. Harold. "Wondering About Spiritual Gifts?" *Focus* 4 (August). 3.

6. Swindoll, 3.

7. Stanley, Charles. *God's Children, Gifted For Ministry.*

8. Coleman Lyman, et al, *Discovering God's Will: Gifts & Calling.* Littleton, CO: Serendipity House, 1998. 6.

9. *Life Application Study Bible*, p. 1958.

10. Zodhiates Spiros. *Greek Dictionary Appendix.* p.7.

In His Presents

Spiritual Gifts

	Romans 12	1 Corinthians 12	Ephesians 4	1 Peter 4	Other Scriptures
What?					
Why?					
To Whom?					
By Whom?					
Important Points					

The "Senior Play":
Public Performers and Prepared Planners

Did you graduate from a small or a large high school? I went to Northside High School in Fort Smith, Arkansas. My graduating class had approximately 600 students. On the other hand, Tommy and our two children all graduated from Bald Knob High School. In each case, their graduating classes had less than 100 students. That is quite a difference. The size of each school carried with it both positives and negatives. I could choose from French, German, Spanish, or Latin when deciding on a foreign language to take. The kids could only take Spanish. They knew the names of everyone with whom they graduated. I had a close group of about eight to ten girls I knew well, another twenty to thirty students who were acquaintances, and after that I might have been able to put the right name to some faces but there was a majority of people I didn't know at all. Upon going back to my ten-, twenty-, and thirty-year reunions, (Okay, so I'm old!) there were some people I don't think I had ever seen in my life.

In His Presents

When Tommy and I started our teaching careers in McCrory, Arkansas, I had my first experience with a small school. I loved it! Each teacher was assigned as a sponsor to a particular class. We worked on everything from floats and money-making projects to the junior/senior play. The neat thing about it was that everyone got involved. All of the students and teachers had something they could do, something for which they were responsible.

Just imagine with me, if you will, that all of us are students in a very small high school that puts on a senior play every year. The rules state that every senior has to take part in some way in the production of the play. There are four possible crews you can be part of and you must choose the one that best suits you.

Your choices include being one of the *stars on stage*. You could be up front saying your lines, performing for the audience. If that doesn't melt your butter, maybe you would be part of the *directing team*. You would be in charge of organizing the play itself, choosing which play you do, selecting the best people for each part, and directing the practices and format of the play.

If neither of these appeal to you, how about being part of the *stage crew*? These are the people who are behind the scenes getting things done. They have the props and costumes ready for each act; they close and open the curtains; they help the whole play run like clockwork.

If being the star, the director, or the stage crew doesn't fall into your comfort zone, then maybe you would prefer being in the *audience*. Before you get too excited about this position and think it means you have nothing to do but to sit and watch, then think again! Remember, you are part of the class that is putting the play on for your community. As an audience member, your classmates need you to critique what is being done, to make sure the lines are said correctly and that everything goes smoothly. You are also their cheer-leader, so to speak. You encourage and motivate them to keep trying.

So, which one is it? You have to choose one group. Are you the star, the director, the stage crew, or the audience? Have you decided? If you are true to yourself and your God-given personality, then you have probably just determined your area of the spiritual gifts.

You see, the church operates in much the same way as that senior play. It needs the *Public Proclaimers,* those who are willing to be out front and to vocally share with others. It also needs the *Prepared Planners* who have the vision of the task at hand, see what needs to be done, and how to organize others so it is accomplished. The church must also have *Private Performers,* the behind-the-scenes people who take care of the details and work to help everything run smoothly but are rarely seen. And then, finally, there needs to be *Profound Perceivers,* those who discern what is right and wrong with the production and encourage those who are more out in front.

As you peruse these four categories, does something sound slightly familiar? Does it bring to mind the four different personalities we discussed in previous chapters? Can't you just see the Popular Sanguine being the star on stage, the out-front kind of person? Where is the Powerful Choleric? This personality was just made to be the director, the one who plans and organizes what everyone needs to do. Then there is the Perfect Melancholy who takes care of all of the details and behind-the-scenes activities just as the stage hand would do. Don't forget the Peaceful Phlegmatic who makes a perfect audience and can be there to critique and encourage.

Isn't God good? He is the One Who gave us our uniqueness. He is the One Who handpicks our spiritual gifts. He usually will give us gifts that are conducive to our personality. Remember, though, if He doesn't gift us according to our personality, then He will equip us for our ministry. So don't worry about where your comfort zone lies. Just trust and obey!

Public Proclaimers

The Public Proclaimers are the ones who share God's Word in the public arena. They are usually in a more noticeable position and what they do is more obvious and in the forefront. When looking at the list of spiritual gifts from our four passages of scripture discussed in Chapter 8, there are probably four of the gifts that could be considered public proclaimer gifts. These include prophecy, evangelism, teaching, and the word of wisdom.

Prophet. The prophet is very *truth oriented*. When we think of Old Testament prophets, we usually think of them as being people who would *foretell* what would happen. They did this, but they also were *forth* tellers. They proclaimed or told forth God's word to the people of their day. What they had to share were sometimes hard, unpopular, yet urgent messages that spoke to the sins of the people. They would warn the people of impending judgment should they not repent. This means they sometimes came across as being harsh, insensitive people.

Their standard was God's word, no more, no less. They based their message on *"thus saith the LORD"* and were painfully direct in addressing the shortcomings and needs of the people. Let's just say they probably didn't make the most popular list, but that was okay with them because it was God to whom they were accountable, not man.

More than likely you know people who are like this today. People who can quickly assess a situation and then speak up to confront a wrong. They have public boldness and don't mind calling the kettle black whenever and wherever it is necessary.

The New Testament had its share of prophets. John the Baptist confronted the ruler of his day about an adulterous relationship he was having with his sister-in-law. Peter confronted Ananias and Sapphira when they lied to the church. Paul spoke out against Peter at the Jerusalem council when he tried to backpedal on requiring believers to keep the Jewish law.

We also have modern-day prophets: Randall Terry of Operation Rescue, Phyllis Schaffly of Eagle Forum, and our own Brother Jurl Mitchell. These are people whose gift it is to address the truth, set forth the truth, and confront others when they are ignoring the truth. Look closely. You have prophets in your church. Maybe you have misunderstood them. Maybe you have resented them when you were the recipient of their confrontation. Maybe you *are* the prophet and have sometimes stayed quiet because what you have to say seems too harsh. The church needs prophets, people who will keep us on line and in line and will do so in a way that is honoring to God.

Evangelist. The evangelist is *soul oriented.* These people have a deep, constant burden for the lost. They can more easily share the gospel, but they can also teach others how to be a more effective witnesses.

If you do not have the gift of evangelism, that does not free you from being a witness for the Lord. The Great Commission was given to all of us. Each of us is meant to be a soul winner; it is just that it comes more easily to those with this gift. They have a burning desire to see people brought to the saving knowledge of Christ. They can and usually do turn any situation into a witnessing opportunity. As Dr. Michael Youssef states it, the gift of evangelism is the "spiritual ability to communicate the gospel message in relevant terms to unbelievers."[1]

Consider Paul on Mars Hill. As he viewed all of the

idolatry in which the people were steeped, *"his spirit was stirred in him"* (Acts 17:16). He used their own altar to the *unknown god* to preach to them about the one true God. Look at Philip. He was having a series of revival services in many Samaritan villages, yet when God sent him to one, single Ethiopian, he went. He started right with the scripture the man was reading and began to preach about Jesus.

Think about the men of our day. Thousands respond to the preaching of Billy Graham. Bill Bright of the Campus Crusade for Christ has used different means to share the Gospel — *The Four Spiritual Laws* tract, the Lighthouse movement, calls to prayer and fasting across our nation, and calls to evangelize America. Dr. D. James Kennedy developed Evangelism Explosion that has been used by Jacksonville Baptist Seminary to train our preachers how to best reach out to others with the gospel of Christ.

One of the evangelists I remember best is Brother Leon Harvey. He has been to our church several times for revival meetings and one of the things that amazed me most about this man was how he witnessed to everyone. It might be a waitress in a restaurant or a fellow passenger in the hospital elevator, but they weren't going to get out of his presence until he found out whether or not they knew Christ as personal Savior.

Teacher. While the prophet is truth oriented and the evangelist is soul oriented, the teacher is *concept oriented.* Those with the gift of teaching have the ability to discover and analyze the truth of God's Word and then share its concepts with others in a way they can understand. They truly enjoy studying the Scriptures, researching each passage, and then delivering the message simply, clearly, and accurately.

The New Testament writer Luke had a passion for the facts. He documented the life of Christ and the early church in great detail. He wanted his readers to understand what was going on and to feel as though they were there.

In modern times, we are blessed to have many teachers of God's Word. Adrian Rogers of Bellevue Baptist Church in Memphis, Tennessee, is one of the best at organizing his sermons in outline form. Not only is he systematic in his presentation, but he usually begins each sub topic with words beginning with the same letter or phrases that are parallel in structure. He makes his sermons easy to follow and hard to forget.

Then there is Charles Swindoll. I love to listen to him preach. He is good at incorporating humor, but he is the best at using word pictures. He can tell a story or give an illustration to drive home a point so that it sticks with you. His spiritual gifts illustration about the friend who hadn't opened any of the presents struck my heart. It was a vivid lesson on how we must hurt God's heart when we do the same to the spiritual gifts He gives to us. It is an illustration I'll always remember.

In an earlier chapter, I shared with you how Dr. Harold Cooper had influenced my life as one of my instructors at Central Baptist College. I guess he was the most brilliant man I had ever known or had the privilege to sit under in class. But he never talked down to anyone. He made everyone feel comfortable in his presence. When he preached God's Word, he did it in such a simplistic way that all could understand. That is the mark of a true teacher.

Word of Wisdom. The final gift in the Public Proclaimer category is the gift of the word of wisdom. I can remember Mama telling me that knowledge was simply the accumulation of facts, but wisdom was knowing how to use those facts at the right time and in the right way. That is what these people can do. They are *application oriented*. In other words, they don't just want you to know the concepts of the Bible, they want you to be able to apply them to your own daily life. They teach, preach, and write in such a way as to help us practice what we preach.

These people are practical in their presentation, and they give us practical ways of following what they have taught. Solomon was perhaps the best word-of-wisdom person in the entire Bible. The book of Proverbs is filled with effective, down-to-earth tidbits that we can pull from it pages and put to use immediately in the twenty-first century.

A modern person with the word of wisdom gift is Henry Blackaby. I'm sure many of you have been blessed and motivated by his *Experiencing God* study. Its subtitle is *Knowing and Doing the Will of God*. He doesn't want us to just *know* God's will for our lives, but he gave us practical ways of how we were to go about *doing* His will.

So there you have it, the four Public Proclaimers — those who are out in front teaching, instructing, inspiring, guiding, and witnessing. Did you see yourself in this group? If not, keep reading.

Prepared Planners

Every organization must have leaders, those who see what needs to be done, make the plans to do it, then motivate the troops to accomplish those plans. Prepared Planners are the big picture people. They can envision the end result and can help to organize all it takes to get there.

Leadership. There are two verses that mention these gifts. Romans 12:8 says, *"He that ruleth,* [let him do it] *with diligence."* The Greek word for *ruleth* means "to stand before (in rank); to preside, maintain, be over, rule."[2]

The spiritual gift of ruling is sometimes referred to as leadership. These people are *goal oriented*. They will assume responsibility and leadership if none exist. They know what resources are needed and available to reach the goals. They will move from challenge to challenge and usually want the task finished yesterday.

This role brings with it both responsibility and accountability. People in this position need to realize they are easy targets for criticism. It's always easier to shoot at something in front of you than behind you. Leaders often seem insensitive when delegating and need to remember the church is a group of people with God-given ministries; it is not a to-do list.

Administration. The second scripture that mentions these gifts is 1 Corinthians 12:28. *"God hath set some in the church ... gifts of ... governments."* This occasion is the only occurrence of this word in the New Testament and it means to "steer, pilot, direct."[3]

Most usually refer to the gift described here as that of administration. Where the leader is more goal oriented, the administrator is more *task oriented.* Administrators are self starters and will take care of the details that are necessary to reach the goal. They will help to implement and execute the ideas and plans of the leader.

Since these are two different words in Scripture, some see these as two separate gifts. Others, like Charles Swindoll, view them as two sides of the same coin and define this gift as "the ability to organize and lead projects, to see them through from start to finish, while handling people tactfully and providing the vision to keep them at the task."[4]

Nehemiah illustrates these leadership and administrative gifts. He saw the need to return to his homeland and repair the wall. He enlisted the help of both his superiors and his fellow workers. He gathered materials, assigned tasks, and then fended off the enemy while the people completed their jobs. He kept his eye on the goal and didn't allow the harassment of others to prevent him from doing what he knew had to be done. He was both a leader and administrator.

Paul and Titus must have been a leadership/administration team. In his letter to Titus, Paul tells him to set in order things he had told him (Titus 1:5). Then Paul sets forth in chapters 2 and 3 a list of things for Titus to teach to his members in order for them to live and act appropriately both in the church and in society. Paul had the vision; Titus was to help him carry it out.

When I was taking all of my administration classes before I became a principal, there was always a big discussion as to whether or not the principal was to be a leader or a manager. The distinguishing difference in that case was that a leader was more concerned about the people he was over and how to motivate and inspire them, while a manager was more involved in the day to day operations of the school. I found that both of those tasks were necessary to assure a smooth running school. Both of these are necessary for an effective church as well.

1. Youssef, 30.
2. Zodhiates, 60.
3. Zodhiates, 44.
4. Swindoll, 41.

Author's Note: The spiritual gifts I have mentioned in association with real people in this and upcoming chapters are totally my observation. I have not spoken with any of them concerning what they feel is their spiritual gift. As I understand them, however, the gifts I am trying to describe are exemplified by these people.

Also, I realize that the Old Testament people mentioned were not part of the church. God empowered them for the task He gave them to do, For us, that empowerment comes through the spiritual gifts as they are used within the context of the church.

The "Senior Play": Private Performers and Profound Perceivers

So far we've seen that the Prophet is truth oriented; the Evangelist is soul oriented; the Teacher is concept oriented; the Word of Wisdom gift is application oriented; the Leader is goal oriented; and the Administrator is task oriented.

Before you get too paranoid and think you can't be found in any of these categories, please remember we have two more to go. The first two describe the more public gifts while the remaining two categories are more behind the scenes.

Private Performers

When you see the word *performer* you might automatically think of someone being on stage. In Webster's Dictionary (What would I do without Noah?), that is the secondary meaning of the word. Primarily *perform* means "to carry out; do." The dictionary gives execute, discharge, accomplish, achieve, effect, and fulfill as synonyms.[1] These people get things done. They accomplish the job and they usually do so without being in any part of the limelight. There are four gifts found in this category — service, helps, mercy, and giving.

Service. People with the gift of service are *needs oriented*. The word for service comes from the same root word as *deacon*. It suggests that they assist or support other people in a practical way. Therein lies the source of joy. Their satisfaction comes from assuring that the ministry of the Public Proclaimers or Prepared Planners runs smoothly. As Charles Stanley puts it, "They don't desire attention, they just want to know that what they are doing is needed."[2]

Three New Testament saints manifest the gift of service. Romans 16:1-2 describes Phoebe as a servant of the church and a helper of many, including Paul. Her focus was on filling the needs of other people.

Acts 9:36 records that Dorcas *"was full of good works and almsdeeds."* Almsdeeds referred to the actual helpful action resulting from pity, not just the inner compassion that was felt.[3] She didn't just feel sorry for people; she did something to ease their predicament. The mourners who gathered at her death testified to her care by showing Peter the coats and garments she had made them.

Besides Phoebe and Dorcas, there was also Epaphroditus. Listen to the words Paul used to describe him in Philippians 2 — brother, companion in labor, fellow soldier, your messenger, and *"he ... ministered to my wants"* (verse 25). Evidently, Epaphroditus had been sent by the church at Philippi to deliver money and other items to Paul. While there, he became deathly ill. This didn't stop him from his service to the apostle though. Verse 30 tells us, *"Because for the work of Christ he was nigh unto death, not regarding his life, to supply your lack of service toward me."* He put others first and carried out his task even when gravely ill.

Helps. People with the gift of helps are also *needs oriented,* but instead of their focus being on helping people, it is on taking care of things. They are concerned with the logistics of the service or activity. They run the sound system, set up tables, clean the sanctuary, fix the leaky faucet, turn the light and air on before each service and off afterwards. They avoid the red tape and get things done while other people are standing around talking about it.

Their work supports others. Before you decide that sounds rather unglamorous, stop and think. The frame of a building supports the structure. The skeleton supports the body. The vital organs that do so much are never seen, but the outer body that we do see would be dead without their nourishment and support. The same is true in the church. The church body would be ineffective without the helpers.

We have several at Worden, where I attend. Kathy Delk always makes sure the tables are up, the plates and napkins are bought, and all systems are go for our fellowship meals. Paula Knight sends cards, buys flowers, and organizes food for funerals and such. David Howell does it all. We never see him do things, we just always know it gets done, and usually, it is David that does it. One of our younger men, Brian Coles, overheard us asking how in the world we were going to get all of those spider webs off of our church siding. That afternoon he came over with a high-powered hose and sprayed them down. We all gave David the credit and didn't learn until later that Brian had done the deed.

See what I mean? These people don't care if they are noticed, they just want to help and to know that what they are doing needs to be done. Evelyn Coles takes care of the flower beds. Edna Watson and Tammie Howell decorate for all of our events. The two main men in my life, Tommy and Jared, both have this gift. The only time Jared didn't readily stay and clean up after an event was at his own wedding. We could never get along without these people.

Mercy. People with the gift of mercy are the heart of

the church. They are *feelings oriented.* They show more than sympathy; they have empathy. While sympathy feels *for* others, empathy feels *with* others. That makes a big difference. When others are sad, they cry with them. When others are happy, they laugh with them. They do both sincerely. They give warmth, hope, and comfort to those around them.

We have several merciful people at our church. Shirley Wallace can just sense when someone is in need, and without a word, she'll ease over to them after a service and give them a big hug. Our pastor's wife, Bonnie Goodwin, always has her tissues close, because hurting and crying people usually find their way to her. She is everyone's shoulder to cry on both at church and at school where she is the Gifted and Talented teacher.

My daughter, Jill, has this gift. On Mama's seventy-fifth birthday, we found out she had a brain tumor. She went into the hospital for tests, and the whole family was there to rally around her. She did several funny things during the short month that she lived, but she was terribly disoriented both in the hospital and at Jenny's house where we took her to die.

Jill was tremendously sweet and understanding the entire time. When Mama thought she saw spiders all over the wall, I tried to tell her she was confused. Jill, instead, went over to the wall and began smashing all of the imaginary spiders for her Mimi. When Mama thought the hospital room was a not-so-nice hotel, I tried to tell her she was in the hospital. Jill, instead, played along and took her on walks down the *hotel* hall. I was concerned with the practical. Jill was concerned with the person. And so it is with the gift of mercy.

I don't know, but I think the apostle John must have been a merciful person. Feelings were important to him. And after all, wouldn't you want someone loving and thoughtful to care for your mother if you were dying? Jesus did; that's why He picked John.

Giving. Every church needs a cheerful giver or two. These people are *cause oriented*. They usually, but not always, have the capacity to make money and then find true joy in giving to help others. Once again, please note that if you do not have the spiritual gift of giving, that does not mean that God does not expect you to give of your tithes and offerings to Him. It is just that these people go above and beyond.

Charles Swindoll says, "Giving spontaneously, generously, and always with a cheerful attitude, they even shock us sometimes by offering a gift far beyond what was needed or requested."[4] If there is a financial need, they fill it. If someone needs food, clothes, or transportation, these people see to it that they have it. The key to this gift is that it is all usually done in secret. They don't give for show, they have no hidden motives. They simply enjoy meeting the material needs of people and organizations.

My daddy had the gift of giving as I noted in my Christmas coat story. There were many other times he provided clothes, food, and money to people in need, even when they were complete strangers.

The widow who gave her last mite, gave what she had out of love to the Lord. Not always does the giver have an abundance of means. They are never afraid, however, to share what they have with others. The widow at Zarephath fed Elijah her last meal. As a result, the Lord gave her a full supply of oil. Barnabas, *"Having land, sold it, and brought the money, and laid it at the apostles' feet"* (Acts 4:37). They all shared what they had of earthly goods for a heavenly cause.

Profound Perceivers

We are now down to our last category. If you are not a Public Proclaimer, a Prepared Planner, or a Private Performer, maybe you are one of the Profound Perceivers, the audience for our senior play.

Remember, I explained that being part of this audience didn't mean just sitting and watching. Instead, it carried with it more of the essence of critiquing the work. That doesn't mean being critical of what everyone else is doing. It means helping them to fine tune their activities.

There are four spiritual gifts in this category — discernment, faith, word of knowledge, and exhortation. The first three of these are *truth oriented*. If you will remember, the prophet is also truth oriented. The prophet speaks forth the truth in a public arena, but these gifts are more private. They function better on a more individual basis or in one-on-one situations.

The word *perceive* gives a better indication of what I'm talking about. It means "to attain awareness or understanding." *Perception*, a form of the word, means "insight, or a capacity for comprehension."[5] These people observe others and their actions and seem to have insight into their motives.

Discernment. Those with the gift of discernment can clearly distinguish between truth and error. They try the spirits, so to speak, and can detect false teachers. They are usually the ones to clearly see God's will and direction in spiritual matters.

Paul instructed members in the churches of both Galatia and Corinth to test what they heard against Scripture to be sure they were not being taught erroneous doctrine. Peter could detect the lying spirit of both Ananias and Sapphira when they agreed to tell the church they had sold their land for less than they actually had. When the damsel with the spirit of divination followed Paul around proclaiming him to be a servant of the most high God, he knew that although her information was correct, her source was a demon and he performed an exorcism on the spot.

The church needs discerners to detect subtle errors and deficiencies in the truth.

Faith. Each of us who is a child of God was given a portion of faith in order that we might accept what Christ did on the cross as a means of our redemption. People who have the gift of faith have the ability to believe God above and beyond what is shown in the daily Christian walk. Charles Swindoll states, "We can define this gift as the ability to discern God's will, pursue it with extraordinary confidence, and then lay hold of God's promises with remarkable results."[6]

Paul exhibited this kind of faith in Acts 27 when his ship faced certain destruction. He, with confidence, told his fellow passengers that no one would lose his life, but the ship would be lost. He knew God meant for him to stand before Caesar and an angel had told him that no one would lose their life because of the storm. He accepted God's will and direction wholeheartedly and was able to encourage others by doing so.

In more modern times, the story of George Mueller best illustrates a person with the gift of faith. Every aspect of the orphanage run by Mueller and his wife was a total work of faith. Some said he would never share a need or a burden with anyone except the Lord and then in faith wait for the answer. One such time occurred when he and the children sat down to an empty table for a meal. There was no food on the table because there was no food in the house. As they gathered for the meal, Mr. Mueller, as always, gave thanks for what the Lord would provide. In the middle of the prayer, there was a knock at the door. The milkman was standing there because his milk cart had broken down right in front of the orphanage. He knew the milk would spoil before he could make arrangements to get it into town, so he asked Mr. Mueller if he would have any use for all of that milk. That was faith! God honored his faith, and I'm sure many lives were touched and encouraged as a result of this one man's confidence in God.

Word of Knowledge. People with this gift find joy and motivation in study. They seek truth for themselves because they truly want to know what God is saying. These people spend a great deal of time in prayer and in God's Word. They will truly dig for the truth. People will then seek them out because of their greater understanding of what God is saying. Such study enables them to encourage others in the Christian walk.

Kay Arthur comes to mind when I think of this gift. Probably more than any other person, Mrs. Arthur has taught people the method for truly getting into God's word and gleaning its truth for themselves. Her inductive Bible studies, and *Precept upon Precept* classes have made God's word approachable and understandable to people who wouldn't have tried to study it before.

Exhortation. Last, but not least, is the gift of exhortation. The word for exhortation is the same word that is used for the Holy Spirit. It indicates one who comes to another's side to assist, help, or encourage. People with this gift seek to motivate and support others and to enable them to move forward in their Christian life.

Exhorters have the ability to see the steps of action that are necessary to lead others to maturity. They can visualize the potential spiritual achievement of people and will confront individuals when necessary to spur them toward this goal.

They also have the ability to bring harmony between diverse parties. Barnabas was an exhorter to John Mark, and Paul was an exhorter to Timothy.

You may have noticed that some of the Biblical characters were mentioned several times in the list of gifts. That is because the Holy Spirit gives everyone at least one spiritual gift, but many times more than one.

Please be aware that we should never sit around and not do something simply because it is not our gift. *"Whatsoever thy hand findeth to do, do it with thy might"* (Ecclesiastes 9:10). No matter what or how many gifts you have, remember they were given to you by God for His glory and the edification and strengthening of His church. May we never be guilty of leaving our gifts in the box!

Unwrapping the Gift

This spiritual gifts inventory was adapted from one I found on the Internet three years ago. I removed some statements and reworded others to make this more applicable to our study. This exercise is for both Chapters 9 and 10 and is meant to be a tool for helping you determine your own spiritual gift.

Spiritual Gifts Discovery Tool[7]

Mark each of the following 70 statements according to the following rating scale.

0 — completely disagree
1 — disagree somewhat
2 — can't decide
3 — agree somewhat
4 — strongly agree

_____ 1. I like to proclaim God's word to fellow Christians.

_____ 2. It is a joy for me to proclaim God's plan of salvation to unchurched people.

_____ 3. I'm excited in helping people to discover important truths in the Scripture.

_____ 4. It is enjoyable to motivate people to a higher spiritual commitment.

_____ 5. People with spiritual problems seem to come to me for advice and counsel.

_____ 6. I received excellent grades in school.

_____ 7. There is great joy in doing little jobs around the church.

___ 8. I look for opportunities to assist people in their work.

___ 9. There is great joy in leading people to accomplish group goals.

___ 10. I like to organize people for more effective ministry.

___ 11. There is great satisfaction in giving large amounts of money for the Lord's work.

___ 12. I feel great compassion for the problems of others.

___ 13. It seems easy to perceive whether a person is honest or dishonest.

___ 14. I am ready to try the impossible because I have a great trust in God.

___ 15. I like to proclaim the Word of God to comfort others.

___ 16. I seem able to determine when the Spirit has prepared a person to receive Christ.

___ 17. Teaching a Bible class is one of the most enjoyable things I could do in church.

___ 18. It is a joy to give encouragement to people who are discouraged.

___ 19. I enjoy providing solutions to difficult problems in life.

___ 20. It seems easy to learn difficult truths.

___ 21. I enjoy doing routine tasks for the glory of God.

___ 22. I enjoy helping with the emergency tasks around the church.

___ 23. People seem to enjoy following me in doing an important task.

___ 24. There is joy in making important decisions.

___ 25. I find real joy in giving a generous portion of my money to the Lord.

___ 26. Visiting people in retirement homes gives me great satisfaction.

___ 27. I seem to know very quickly whether something is right or wrong.

___ 28. When things seem impossible, I'm ready to move forward.

___ 29. I enjoy relating God's Word to the issues of the day.

___ 30. I feel a burden to share the gospel with people.

___ 31. It seems that people learn when I teach them.

___ 32. I like to encourage inactive church members to become involved Christians.

___ 33. It seems that people generally follow my advice.

___ 34. I am able to understand difficult portions of God's Word.

___ 35. I receive great satisfaction in doing small or seemingly trivial tasks in church.

___ 36. I desire to do the tasks which will free others for their ministry.

___ 37. It is more effective to delegate a task to someone else rather than to do it myself.

___ 38. I enjoy the responsibility for the achievement of group goals.

___ 39. I appreciate the opportunity to financially support a critical situation.

___ 40. I sense joy in comforting people in difficult situations.

___ 41. The difference between truth and error is easily perceived by me.

___ 42. I'm often ready to believe God will lead us through a situation when others feel it is impossible.

___ 43. It is important for me to speak God's word of warning and judgment in the world today.

___ 44. It is a joy to share what Jesus means to me with an unchurched neighbor.

___ 45. One of the joys of my ministry is training people to be more effective Christians.

___ 46. People who are feeling perplexed often come to

me for encouragement and comfort.

___ 47. I feel that I have special insight in selecting the best alternative in a difficult situation.

___ 48. I have a clear understanding of Biblical doctrines.

___ 49. I find more satisfaction in doing a job than finding someone else to do it.

___ 50. I appreciate a ministry of helping other people to bear their burdens.

___ 51. It is a thrill to inspire others to greater involvement in church work.

___ 52. The development of effective plans for church ministry gives me great satisfaction.

___ 53. It is a joy to see how much money I can give to the Lord.

___ 54. I enjoy ministering to a person who is sick in the hospital.

___ 55. I can judge well between the truthfulness and error of a given theological statement.

___ 56. People seem to view me as one who believes everything is possible.

___ 57. It seems essential to me to share God's Word even if it irritates others.

___ 58. I feel a deep concern for the unreached people in my community.

___ 59. It is easy to organize materials for teaching a Bible class.

___ 60. I would rather call on a delinquent family in my church than an unchurched family.

___ 61. I have a strong sense of confidence in my solutions to problems.

___ 62. It is an exciting challenge to read and study a difficult book of the Bible.

___ 63. I like to do things without attracting much attention.

___ 64. If a family is facing a serious crisis, I enjoy the opportunity to help them.

___ 65. There is great satisfaction in having others follow me in performing tasks.

___ 66. I would rather make decisions for the group than persuade them to reach the same decision.

___ 67. I can give sacrificially because I know that God will meet my needs.

___ 68. It is a special satisfaction to visit people who are confined to their homes.

___ 69. I often seek the motives of a person and look beneath the words.

___ 70. When people are discouraged, I enjoy giving them a positive vision.

The Discovery Tool Profile Sheet

Transfer your scores for each question onto the following table, then compute the sum of each row. This provides your score for each gift.

Prophet   1.____ 15.____ 29.____ 43.____ 57.____ =_____

Evangelist   2.____ 16.____ 30.____ 44.____ 58.____ =_____

Teacher   3.____ 17.____ 31.____ 45.____ 59.____ =_____

Exhortation 4.____ 18.____ 32.____ 46.____ 60.____ =_____

Wisdom   5.____ 19.____ 33.____ 47.____ 61.____ =_____

Knowledge   6.____ 20.____ 34.____ 48.____ 62.____ =_____

Helps   7.____ 21.____ 35.____ 49.____ 63.____ =_____

Serving   8.____ 22.____ 36.____ 50.____ 64.____ =_____

Leadership   9.____ 23.____ 37.____ 51.____ 65.____ =_____

Administration	10.____ 24.____ 38.____ 52.____ 66.____ =_____

Administration　　10.____　24.____　38.____　52.____　66.____　=_____

Giving　　11.____　25.____　39.____　53.____　67.____　=_____

Mercy　　12.____　26.____　40.____　54.____　68.____　=_____

Discernment　　13.____　27.____　41.____　55.____　69.____　=_____

Faith　　14.____　28.____　42.____　56.____　70.____　=_____

In the spaces below, list your gifts from highest to lowest score beginning on dominant side.

Dominant　　　　Subdominant

_____　　_____

_____　　_____

_____　　_____

_____　　_____

_____　　_____

_____　　_____

_____　　_____

1. Webster, 627.
2. Stanley.
3. Zodhiates, 911.
4. Swindoll, 40.
5. Webster, 625, 626.
6. Swindoll, 49.
7. Spiritual   Gifts   Discovery   Tool.   http://www.cforc.com/offline.html

Presenting Our Presents

$Look$ around you, ladies. Your church is full of natural talent. Many can sing or play a musical instrument. Others are artistic and have creative abilities. Some may be natural athletes or mechanics. But right now I want you to think about one of your own natural talents.

As I shared with you in the forward of this book, my talent was mostly in the musical arena. As I take you through the progression I followed to find and develop this ability, I want you to think how this applies to the cultivation of any skill.

It all began when I expressed an *interest* in taking piano lessons. That was a challenge because we didn't have a piano! I had always enjoyed music and singing, so the next step for me was to learn how to read music. When we moved from North Little Rock to Little Rock, Mama found a piano teacher just two blocks from our home. The school was between our house and hers, so I could easily walk back and forth to lessons. My parents even purchased an old upright piano for me to practice on. I was set and ready.

I took my lessons very seriously. I wanted to learn all I could about the different notes, the lines and spaces, the time value of the notes, everything. I immersed myself in the information Miss Brickhouse (that was really her name) gave me. I was spending time absorbing all the *insights* into the rudiments of music.

Then came the *involvement*. I practiced and practiced and practiced some more. My teacher told me I should practice at least thirty minutes a day. In the beginning, I practiced even more because I really wanted to learn. But little by little, the practice became more of a chore instead of a joy. It was not fun anymore, and I did not willingly go to the piano each day as I had at first. Then came those famous words that mothers always say, "Someday, you'll be glad I made you practice and keep taking lessons." She was right, of course, but at the time, I certainly didn't think so.

We soon moved to Fort Smith, and I thought this would be a good time to quit my lessons. Mother had a different idea. Instead of scaling back (Pardon the pun!), we stepped up to a higher playing field. I began taking classical piano from two of the best teachers in the state. My lessons went from thirty minutes to one hour, and with the increase in lesson time, came the increased expectation that my daily practice would extend to an hour as well.

I went from playing for enjoyment to playing for competitions. More and more, I received *input* from others. My teachers would critique me. Once a year they would have out-of-state judges come to their home and grade my performance. Then, came the concerto competitions. I would be on one piano, my teacher on another, and I would compete in front of a panel of judges for the chance to play with the Fort Smith Symphony. I was always grateful that I never won because I would've died of fright if I had ever had to do that!

Little by little there were more and more *indicators* that others thought I had musical abilities as well. I was asked to play in certain places and for certain events. I was only in the sixth grade when I became church pianist and played at a wedding for the first time. (Trust me, they weren't too picky!) I was petrified, but the more I played, the more comfortable it became and the more satisfaction I received from the experience.

Today, I am so thankful that Mama made me keep going. In fact, I wish I could still play all of those classical pieces that I could once do from memory. Now I receive great satisfaction from still being church pianist and only wish I could play the hymns with more freedom and expression. I wish I had listened more to all of the music theory so I could transpose the keys and go from one song to another with ease. I had discovered and developed my gift, but did I do all that I could?

You probably went through the same thing in developing your natural talent. First you showed *interest*, then you gleaned *insight* by finding out all that you could about that area. You became more and more *involved*, and as a result, received *input* from others and satisfaction within yourself. Finally, there were *indicators* to show where your strengths and weaknesses lay.

Ladies, just as we were born with natural talents and potentials at our physical birth, I hope you now realize that we were reborn having gifts of the Spirit at our spiritual birth. It is now our duty and responsibility toward God to find our spiritual gift, open it, and present it back to Him so He can use it for the perfecting of the saints, the work of the ministry, and the edifying of the body of Christ.

How do you go about finding your gift? It is much the same progression I went through in learning to play the piano.

Determine Your Area of Interest

What do you want to do? What do you enjoy doing? What brings you pleasure, satisfaction, and fulfillment?

Where do you feel needed? To what area of service do you feel drawn? What age group or category of people do you feel compelled to be around and help or serve in some way? These questions should help direct you to the area of your spiritual gift.

Develop an Abundance of Insight

It is important that you study and try to find out all that you can about the gifts. The best place to start is, of course, the Scriptures. Concentrate on the gift passages that we have studied: Romans 12, 1 Corinthians 12, Ephesians 4, 1 Peter 4. Use your Bible dictionary and concordance. Research the background of these passages. Study our chart that coordinates the verses according to the *from whom, to whom, what,* and *why* questions.

Next, pray. Accept by faith that you are gifted. To doubt this is a sin. Either you're gifted or the Bible is untrue. Simply ask God to reveal the gift He has for you. He wants you to know. He doesn't say, "Here's a gift, but don't open it. You must try to guess what it is."

1 John 5:14-15 tells us, *"This is the confidence that we have in him, that, if we ask any thing according to his will, he heareth us: and if we know that he hear us, whatsoever we ask, we know that we have the petitions that we desired of him."* Trust me, it is His will that you know your area of giftedness and use it, so *ask* Him!

Dr. E. Harold Henderson used the verse in James 4:3 to tie in with the spiritual gifts. *"Ye ask, and receive not, because ye ask amiss, that ye may consume it upon your lusts."* His comments on this verse were, "God will reveal the spiritual gift of the person who is available to exercise it. However, He does not reveal anything to one who wants to satisfy curiosity but has no commitment to serve."[1] Ask, ladies, but be ready to put it into action when God reveals your gift. Increased knowledge means increased accountability.

There is a myriad of books and tapes on this subject by various speakers and authors. I would suggest any of the studies by Kay Arthur, Charles Swindoll, Michael Youssef, or Adrian Rogers. There are even books on individual gifts such as service, leadership, faith, encouragement, evangelism, and effective Bible teaching. Ask your pastor for some suggestions or check your church library or a local Christian bookstore.

Decide on Arenas of Involvement

Charles Swindoll said, "The only way to find [your spiritual gift] is to jump into ministry of all kinds. Just as it's easier to steer a moving car, it will be easier for you to discover your gifts by trying out a variety of ministries."[2]

I don't know, but if your church is like ours there are all kinds of opportunities available right now. There may be a class that needs a teacher, or someone may need to start a card or hospital visitation ministry. Perhaps they need help in keeping the nursery or setting up and cleaning up for fellowship meals. Maybe your GMA counselors could use some more ears for listening to verses. Maybe there are areas of service that aren't official but have to be done. The flower beds need cleaning; the church sign needs changing; greeters and ushers are needed for each service. On and on the list could go.

Just maybe the Lord has laid a ministry on your heart that your church doesn't have yet. Maybe you feel led toward drama or sign language presentations. Perhaps you could start a homebound ministry or a divorce recovery class. What about career assistance for people or financial stewardship programs? The possibilities are as numerous as the people in your area of influence.

If the Lord has shown you a need, there is a reason. If the Lord has burdened your heart, there is a reason.

Step out in faith. Seek wise counsel. Talk to your pastor, then try your wings. You may be surprised what the Lord can do through you. Remember, "Discovering our gifts shouldn't be an end in itself ... the process doesn't bear fruit unless we act on what we've learned. *The only way we can confirm and develop our gifts is by using them.*"[3] (Italics, mine.)

Desire Assurance Through Indicators

What do you do in service for the Lord that brings you peace and satisfaction? Personal satisfaction isn't the main goal of our spiritual gifts, but the Lord will bring internal indicators that help us to know we are in the right place. Where do you feel at home serving?

There have been some things I agreed to do that ended up being as painful as pulling teeth. It was a chore to face the job each and every time. Other positions were a pleasure. I would look forward to them each week. There have been still other things that I really enjoyed for a while, but when my time was over for that particular job, the joy left.

Be sensitive to God's spirit. Although your gifts don't change, the ones He may bring to the forefront may differ from time to time. And when there is a fit, you will know it. There will be internal indicators that are unmistakable.

Other authors have put it different ways. "Experiment with various gifts. If it is your gift, then you will do it *easily, joyfully, and effectively.*"[4] (Italics, mine.) "Did I find *fulfillment and joy?* Would it be *difficult for me to refrain from serving* there in the future?"[5] (Italics, mine.)

Detect Affirmation Through Input

Just as there are internal indicators when we have found our niche, there will also be external indicators that show we're in the right place. What seems to garnish results? Where has God given you the greatest success? In what areas do other people affirm what you have done?

Dr. Henderson says we should ask, "Were others profited? Did it promote spiritual growth? Did it promote unity? In what areas do others look to you for help? Where do they express the greatest blessing received from you?"[6]

The *Serendipity* study guide puts it this way, "It is helpful to receive the input of those who know us concerning the gifts and strengths they see in us. Fellow believers can assist us in clarifying our gifts."[7]

Charles Stanley said when we find and exercise our gift, "There will be a greater depth to your life and ministry. What we say and do will be more meaningful. People will recognize a maturity in our life ... more power, influence, fruitfulness, and productivity."[8]

Don't be afraid to ask for the input of others. Instead, seek out those who will honestly help you evaluate your strengths as they see them. Remember, the first deacons were chosen based on the qualities other people noted in their lives.[9]

Decipher Your Abilities Through Inventories

The spiritual gift discovery tool that I included in Chapter 10 is one of many that can be used to help clarify your gifts. Many books on the subject will contain inventories that coincide with the way the gifts are presented in the material. Others may be ordered separately and information for doing so is often found on the tape series by particular people or are available through the Internet.

Please remember, these are just tools. They can help get you pointed in the right direction, but let God be your guide. Then allow the internal and external indicators to fine tune the direction you should follow.

Don't take a church job just because no one else will

do it. Take a church job because that is what God wants you to do. I have often said I had rather see a church have only three or four classes taught by spiritually gifted teachers, than to have a class for each age group manned by people who feel they have to be there because no one else will take the position. As a result, many read to their class every Sunday.

What are you doing now that someone else can do, so you can do what God has called you to do? It sounds like a confusing sentence, but it is an important one to consider. Give it some thought and respond accordingly.

Never be envious of another person's gifts. Remember, it is by God's grace that we have differing gifts (Romans 12:6). He gives us the gifts *He* wants us to have, not the ones we request (1 Corinthians 12:11). We must do all that we can to walk worthy of the part the Lord has given us to play in His church. He doesn't want children tossed to and fro. We can prevent this wishy-washy state by growing in Christ (Ephesians 4:15). According to the context of this verse, growth is accomplished by exercising the spiritual gifts.

I'm afraid we have too often given little credence to this topic. We've viewed the gifts simply as a nice little Bible study, or a good theme for a conference talk or a book. We must begin to see this as vital part of our life in Christ.

We will never truly be fulfilled, we will never truly feel complete, we will never truly experience the joy that God meant for us to have until we find our place of service within His church. May we take to heart Paul's instruction to Timothy to not neglect the gift, but instead, "stir it up." Rekindle the flame, and keep it active always.

How blessed we are! Look back over all of the gifts bestowed upon us by our heavenly Father. He gave us our position in Christ. He gave us our unique person-